Quantum Selling

By

Dr Yates J Canipe

Published by

Straightforward Inc, 2259 Old Highway 70, Durant OK 74701

I am Dr. Yates J. Canipe. Welcome. How should one share his background while being entertaining, yet enlightening and inspiring at the same time? You are reading thoughts of a 70 year old, retired, business man, who being bored and wanting to engage the next generation, walked into the Business School at Southeastern Oklahoma State University in early in 2011 after being encouraged by the SOSU Soccer Club to do so. I began teaching at Southeastern that fall. Credentials include a BA in Math and Physics from University of Texas, Austin; a MS and PhD in Meteorology from Texas A&M, College Station, and a MBA from University of California at Dominguez Hills. As a side note, certifications in Neuro Linguistic Programming (NLP), Silva Mind Control, Huna, Holographic Memory Resolution and other studies of the mind serve as a focused hobby now.

Joining the Air Force at age 17 as a high school dropout led to many promotions and ultimate retirement as a Major. The next 30 years I spent running large organizations in most aspects and going independent by starting several companies which included raising $10.5 Million in Venture Capital for one of them.

My last book "Quantum Huna" was published in January 2013.

Table of Contents

CHAPTER 1 - INTRODUCTION QUANTUM
SELLING

1.1 - EVERY SALE IS BASED ON EMOTION (ENERGY)

As one would say, "True Learning is not a linear process." Thus, this book is also not linear. It is up to you to figure out why, later. The very structured linear person may like the interior of the book while the creative person may like discovering what comes next. Now, I once heard from a somewhat famous person that, "Things don't change until you change." So in an effort to get you to change NOW, the following is an absolutely enjoyable exercise and is extremely important for reasons that you will discover more and more as you do the exercise over and over. It is my opinion that your success is directly tied to your ability to make the words and phrases on the flash cards in the appendices a part of your everyday conversation. And you are welcome to it. They will become a natural part of a new you.

Ready for an adventure? You can do this by yourself or with another person. 1. Take the Quantum Selling Flash Cards and separate the Conscious By-Pass Phrases and the Priority Command Verbs from the other cards and make a deck of just these cards. 2. Shuffle the cards. 3. Pick a subject you like, such as a hobby or anything else that you currently have some interest in. How surprised will you be to find that anyone can pick the subject, any subject, and it doesn't make any difference? 4. Start talking about the subject or topic. 5. Look at the top card on the deck and incorporate that word or phrase into your train of thought as you continue to talk. 6. Place the card on the bottom of the deck. 7. Repeat Steps 5 and 6 until the deck is exhausted.

While doing this exercise, notice how you feel about the subject or topic. If another person is doing it with you, notice how they are responding.

Pick another subject or topic and do the exercise again and NOW again.

The subject can be anything from collecting beer cans; to selling corporate bonds; to fine art of the seventeenth century; to what you would do in your wildest dreams. JUST pick a topic, any topic, and shuffle the cards.

After you do this exercise, then read the book or watch the DVDs, then watch the DVDs or read the book. It is not the Bible or the Truth. It is only my opinion; and sometimes I forget which is which. So do the exercises, practice, have fun with it and notice the good things that happen.

1.2 – Projecting

One of the most difficult and frustrating things for a salesman or sales manager to do is to debrief or give feedback to a salesman after the sales call. This is true, also, in the broader sense of online sales or selling an audience whether it is live or via video. There is one principle that you as a person, sales person or as a sales manager can use. This is the Quantum principle that we are ALL connected. You may also hear it discussed somewhat as "You get what you project." You are always projecting. There is always an energy field around you, the strength and character of which you control. You may pull that field in closer to your body or extend it out further from your physical body. The information or intelligence contained within that field is also directly controlled by you, if not consciously then unconsciously. I said, this control may not be your conscious mind. It may be your subconscious mind (and usually is) that has control of the content. You hear the phrase "Content is King" when communication companies are talking about being sustainable over the long haul. Content is King in your field also. Here is an example of how it works in the negative.

You go out on a sales call and you have a MONEY concern. This is your personal concern. You may be behind in a car payment, house payment or some other payment. You may be thinking about the amount of commission you will make if the sale goes through. It does not make any difference what issue or circumstance as long as it is about money.

You can almost be absolutely guaranteed that the client will have a MONEY concern. The product or service will be too expensive. The financial terms are not right. The contract is a high financial risk for the company.

The point is: Your MONEY concern will be sensed and manifested by the potential client as a MONEY concern.

When this is detected as a pattern in several sales calls, then you can be sure that you have a personal problem, or belief, that you need to address. It may be as simple as being able to suspend a limiting belief. Such as "I am not worthy of receiving a $50,000 bonus for this project." The vast majority of objections that come up in sales are the objections **projected** into the situation by the thoughts and beliefs residing in the salesman's head, in your head.

So how do you handle this without therapy, counseling or some other self improvement technique? The easiest way is to learn to stay FOCUSED on the best thing for the client. If you can constantly stay focused on the client's best interest, then over time you will truly learn to serve and recognize when a hidden agenda comes up; and thus be able to adjust your **THINKING**.

This Quantum principle is there in ALL human interactions. If you notice that you turn off certain kinds of people, then you are projecting SOMETHING that those people can detect and to which they react negatively. A typical example is a "Holier Than Thou" or arrogant attitude. People can detect that you REALLY do not like them and therefore, they do not like you. The simple law of reciprocity is in force. This also works in the positive way. If you do not make PRE judgments about people, then you will find that you are acceptable to a lot more people.

1.3 - Your Own Misconceptions Of Selling

What is it?, Who does it? and Why?

We, and I do mean We. That is you and I and everyone else in this world is selling all the time. This is the primary reason for using our developed skills in communication. We are constantly selling our ideas, thoughts, beliefs along with STUFF.

A young man just walked into my office and when I explained the left and right brain to him and what selling really was, he immediately said "Even when I go to the store and buy a loaf of bread?" I said, "YES." During the analysis of him buying that loaf of bread, he revealed that he only bought ONE brand BECAUSE that was the only brand that his son would eat. His son would pitch fits and become very disruptive if he did not get the bread he wanted in the package he recognized. Understand the son did not necessarily recognize the bread by its taste, color, smell or feel. He did recognize something and demanded to see it. The young man had just made an emotional buy; one that had nothing to do with nutrition and everything to do with how it was going to make him feel emotionally.

You can now go online and take exams, quizzes and tests about the dominance of your left or right brain which will be analyzed. The results shown are presented according to different agendas. For example, these exercises say you are more or less creative, more or less logical, more or less intuitive, more or less rational. These are fun to take and appear to be a fairly accurate measure of how you **CURRENTLY** use your brain. To review quickly, the Left Brain is supposed to be the logical or rational side and the Right Brain is supposed to be the creative or intuitive side.

The brain has two sides because we are a bilateral creature. Many studies and examples are available which show that either side of the brain can perform all essential functions. In reality one side of the brain is the backup for the other. Over time, each side has become specialized or dedicated to some functions and CAN DO ALL.

The history of sales training from Zig Zigler to the present has focused on the left, or logical function of the brain; and thus pushes Features and Benefits. You were taught to just keep presenting and focusing on data and numbers and you will succeed. This worked in the absence of anything else and people were told that their buying decision must be logical. You will get an explanation that. This is NOT true.

1.4 - The Typical Salesman Image

Take your own survey; it will confirm for you that for most people the first image which comes to the mind when asked to describe a salesman is that of a used car salesman, a fast talker who only cares about the contract being signed.

The immediate task, therefore, is to deal with this image which exists in the minds of most people. So in the profession of selling, the first question (or one of the first) you should ask is, "Have you ever met a salesman that you liked?" The most common answer is NO. Now you know where you stand.

If the answer is NO, your next move is to say, "Never, not even one?" If the answer is still NO, respond with the following.

"Well, if there was a salesman you liked what would he or she be like? What characteristics would they have? How would they treat you?"

Then listen, and you had better do what they say.

NOW, if they happen to say YES, you already know what to say.

What is it about that salesperson (those salespeople) that you liked? What characteristics did they have? How did they treat you? What made them different?

Then LISTEN, and you had better conform to their belief and follow through with that behavior. You may make a sale without doing this, but chances are it will be the only one with them; and it may come apart after it appears to be done. This is called buyers' remorse.

This process of determining the environment or beliefs of the other person or persons is key to any situation where you know or think the other person you are to begin communicating with may be of a different mindset than yourself. For example, you are going in for an interview. You know that you do not have the total qualifications that the advertisement or job opening description requested. So the first question to ask is, "Have you ever hired someone who did not exactly fit the profile as stated?" Now, based on the answer you know how to proceed.

1.5 - All Sales Are Emotional Decisions

It is a myth that sales occur as logical decisions made after logical, clear presentations of features and benefits. Just stop and think about any buying decision that you have ever made. Thoughts lead to FEELINGS which lead to behavior. You may have looked at the DATA presented but the decision was made because you felt good about it.

Let's examine the connections.

First: Ask, "What do you want" or any variation to understand the end result they desire.

Second: Ask, "Up until NOW, what has kept (prevented) you from getting it (the desired result)?"

Third: Ask, "How are you going to feel once you have it?"

Practice: Using their exact words to express, "So, as soon as you move past what has prevented you, you will be well on your way to having it and having that "ooohhh" feeling, won't you?"

When you encounter an objection.......

IT'S YOUR OBJECTION!

If the prospect has a money or price objection, YOU HAVE AN ISSUE WITH MONEY or PRICE.

Historically, there have been two ways to deal with objections. The first was to keep a list of objections and canned responses. The canned responses may have been someone's experience of what worked or the result of a brain storming session. This is still very popular in cold calling, especially when the calling is done in a phone bank operation. The screen simply shows a list of known objections and responses. The salesperson making the call simply clicks on the screen and reads the canned response.

A second method was developed by Richard Bandler. In this scenario the salesperson knows the objection, or thinks he knows the objection that will present itself. Since he "knows" the future, he inoculates. That is, he brings up the objection before the client does and handles it up front. Most times the same canned answer or some other form of emotional appeal to elitism is used.

What if you presented yourself in such a way that objections never came up? Notice I said presented YOURSELF. If you truly learn and apply the principles here, then objections will simply and quickly fade away or never arise.

1.6 - Decisions and Choices

Let me ask you, "Would you like for a person to _decide_ to buy something from you?" or "Would you like for a person to _choose_ to buy something from you?"

What is the difference? You may have decided to buy a Ford and you have not chosen a dealer. When people choose to do business with you, they and you are acknowledging that competition is involved.

In looking at definitions of "decision" and "choice" we see circular definitions. A "decision" is something somebody has chosen, something that somebody chooses or makes up his or her mind about, after considering it and other possible choices. He made a final decision on the guest list. A choice is the result of choosing something or somebody, a decision to choose one thing, person or course of action in preference to others.

Just looking at the definition implies that there is no difference between decision and choice. I believe there is a _difference_ in the way the mind processes the words today, acknowledging that this may change tomorrow.

Therefore, I assert that when a person makes a decision, then they feel bound to stick to the path selected and justify it in some way. When a person makes a choice, then they DO NOT feel bound to stick to the path selected. I like chocolate ice cream and that is all I will eat, hence the decision. I choose chocolate ice cream because it is my favorite. I may choose something different next time.

The key principle is; successful people make choices, and acknowledge the presence of competition and the need for learning and flexibility.

1.7 – Selling and SAILing through Life

Selling and SAILing through the world as you master:

Sensory **A**cuity **I**n **L**ife.

Sailing is an outstanding and very complete metaphor for **Selling**. I do not know if you know how to sail, yet, I feel confident that you have seen sailing in movies and on television. We can start by noticing that sail boats, all sail boats, are different from other boats. Of course they have sails, AND more importantly, they have what is called the center board. A vessel with sails and no center board is not capable of sailing because it is at the mercy of the wind. The rudder is almost useless in guiding the vessel without the center board. The wind will simply carry the vessel along with it. With no connection via center board to the real world or the water, you are doomed.

In life and selling, your center board is the basic moral principles by which you live. If you have a set of beliefs that says you are a victim then there is a very high probably that you will fail at true selling and life. You may ONLY be able to sell victimhood to other victims. If you have a belief that money is the root of all evil, or the love of money is the root of all evil; AND, you want to be a GOOD person, then you will be limited in your ability to SELL anything for a profit, even yourself. You can also think of this as Honesty, Responsibility and Integrity.

So let us move on with the assumption that you have a good centerboard. One of the things that excites people who sail is the knowledge that each time they go out on the water will be different. Most people began their sailing experience with small crafts in known safe water. They may have one small sail and the water may be shallow without obstacles between them and their destination. Think about the variables with which you must deal when sailing.

There is the wind speed, direction and variability. Most people think getting from point A to point B is a simple straight line task. This hardly ever happens. They assume that, when first presented the task, the wind will simply carry them to their destination. This is a good place to introduce the second principle of sailing (selling), that of tacking. It is not a straight line to get from point A to point B. You must tack. Meaning, for example, if the destination is northeast of your starting position, you may have to sail north, northeast; and then east, northeast to get to your destination. Tacking is the ability to adapt to the real world in real time to get where you want to go. As you introduce more variables into the equation, tacking becomes more complicated and requires more skill and practice.

How do you handle a change in wind direction? How do you navigate a section of shallow water? What do you do about the reefs or sandbars? Think about that storm on the horizon. Are there other vessels in your way?

ALL strategies and tactics will change with the size and design of the craft. A catamaran will be faster and turn quicker that a deep hulled boat. The deep hulled boat will be more stable and handle rough seas better. As you grow, your sailboat will change. It may get bigger with more and larger sails and require a larger crew. Metaphorically, you will continue to improve as your skills and experiences dictate. It is highly unlikely that you will continue to sail in that original vessel once you learn, master and progress as a sailor. How are you sailing through life?

Dr. Lloyd Glauberman was the first person I knew that actually made great use of the sailing metaphor in his products. Scott Bolan, while attending one of my presentation, came up with the pseudonym **SAIL** as **S**ensory **A**cuity **I**n **L**ife because he observed that the best sales persons are the ones who are flexible; and pay attention to their prospects and customers as individuals, as unique entities.

Whether they know it or not, these successful sellers (SAILors) are using their knowledge and skills in "Quantum Selling". I chose to name this book such after "Quantum Huna" which was published earlier and is focused on your being an ENERGY BEING FIRST.

Chapter 2 - Sales / Persuasion Cycle

2.1 Overview

LEARNING HOW TO USE ANYTHING AND EVERYTHING THAT THE PROSPECT GIVES YOU TO TAKE CONTROL OF THE SITUATION AND MOVE IT IN A POSITIVE DIRECTION.

Look, see the words on this page; notice the curiosity about the above statement. GOOD. You can take any response and use it. Examples to follow.

2.2 - Collect & Gather Client Buying Criteria and Strategy

State to be induced: connection, satisfaction, pride, loyalty, smart, logic, State to be fairness

Techniques: Process Questions, Convincer Questions

Value Hierarchy, Meta-Questioning, Good Decisions, Bad Decisions, Committed Decisions, Objection Responses

PRESUPPOSITIONS FOCUSED AT OUTCOME (MIXING IN NEGATION)

What to look for in order to understand the process: Clean Trans-derivational Searches

CLEAR SIGNS OF BEING SPACED-OUT LOOK COMPLETE AND TOTAL RAPPORT

Outcome: Clean Buying Criteria, Sequence Codes and VAK Codes

Outcome: YOU ARE NOW THE CLIENT'S PERFECT BIO-FEEDBACK MACHINE

2.3 - Combine and Package Client Information

Interweaving your Product and or Service into the Sales Presentation or Delivery

State to be induced: Desire, Excitement, Delight, Obsession, Pleasure, Intelligence, Enthusiasm, Compulsion

Techniques: Replay Buying Criteria, Sequence Codes, VAK Codes, Embedded Commands, Recall Past Purchases, Future Pacing

Value Elicitation, Visual Anchors

PRESUPPOSITIONS FOCUSED AT OUTCOME (MIXING IN NEGATION)

What to look for in order to understand the process: Complete agreement, head nodding, And Prospect is finishing your word, leaning towards you, getting into your presentation

Outcome: Prospect is asking to move to the next step, Prospect asks you to buy or sign contract

2.4 - Turn Client into a Sales Representative for YOU

State to be induced: Loyalty, Pride, Pleasure, Commitment

Techniques: *Metaphorical Stories – get commitment to the next step*

Outcome: Prospect enthusiastically tells you ways by which they will or can assist you.

Sign Contract / Take Money / Get Purchase Order

State to be induced: Satisfaction, Pride, Certainty, Commitment, Security

Techniques: *Metaphorical Stories – Ambiguities*

Outcome: Prospect Pays YOU.

By going with this product you're making a statement, a statement that says Sign me up for the future, Sign me up for a better life, and Sign me up to feel healthier.

Chapter 3 Patterns

3.1 - Capture Attention – Get Interest and Attention

Prospect: Expressed any opening objection

You: Stop – Wait – Let's backup for a moment

(STOP - *Breaks State)*

(Wait – is giving the first command)

(Let's back up a moment – leading into new state before objections)

State who you are and why you are calling. Ask permission to talk.

On the phone cold calling or in a presentation:

Prospect: I am satisfied with my present vendor.

You: UNDERSTAND, if there was some area they could improve on, what area quickly comes to the front of your mind now as you think about it?

What we really specialize in is expanding your already existing programs so you can leverage your resources.

Angry Prospect while on the phone cold calling:

Prospect: Any Negative Response

You: Well that's the very reason I'm calling, I only deal with people who have been severely abused. Like us, I understand because people like us don't deserve to be treated like that.

Prospect: I hate Telemarketers

You: Well, that's good, because I'm not a telemarketer.   When would be a good time we could meet and get off the phone?

Prospect: We already do that in-house.

You: Understand. (Relate, reframe, that's what we do)

Prospect: Sam has given strict orders about screening his calls.

You: Great, can you give him a note and …..

You: I can appreciate that. How would you go about getting a phone or in person appointment?

Prospect: Send information care of gatekeeper - ME

You: When you have the information, how do you get it in front of Sam?

TELEPHONE SCRIPT

You: JOHN, MY NAME IS BOB SMITH AND I REPRESENT STRAIGHTFORWARD TO THE TRAINING INDUSTRY. JOHN, IT WILL TAKE ABOUT 60 SECONDS TO EXPLAIN THE PURPOSE OF THIS CALL, IS NOW A CONVENIENT TIME TO TALK?

If the Prospect says: "NO"

You: John, when would be a good time to spend two seconds with me?

(Make sure you follow exactly when and how he says)

If the Prospect says: "YES"

You: Currently, I am working with companies like, "X",   "Y", and "Z", assisting them to reduce cost of employee turnover, increase productivity, and ultimately this positively impacts their bottom-line profits.

What I would like to do is to spend about 15 to 20 minutes with you to discuss ways we may be able to assist your company, ____(RESULTS)____, in some of these areas to meet your immediate business concerns. Would this be something you would like to do?

Buy Instantaneous

Pattern

IN A PRESENTATION:

This pattern is based on stacking a negative and a positive experience.

You: There are only two types of companies that instantaneously buy this product, they immediately buy this product. You see in the last two years we only had about 90 companies contact us who were ready to buy immediately. The first company was going through a tremendous amount of pain. You see, they had an employee who was filing a lawsuit against them.

Have you ever had your house broken into? Well, it's like being raped, violated and it's not pleasant. And the same is true for an organization; it starts with the manager of that employee, and then the director, Vice President, the legal department; and eventually, finally it falls in the lap of Human Resources to appease the whole situation and propose a solution from a legal perspective as well as an organizational perspective. HR already realize that this is the best product on the market. They usually have researched us and naturally have come to the conclusion that this is the best product for them and it will get results.

The other type of companies that buy this product immediately, they buy instantaneously, they are the ones that are already the best. They are already leading their industry and they want to stay on top or want to keep that uniqueness that differentiates them from all their competitors. They realize the only way to be the best is to have the best employees. And they want to be in business 2 to 10 years from now. So the decision is simple, they naturally decide to have this product implemented.

I would rather see you make your decision to go with this product from the perspective of possibility and not necessity.

A lot of companies ask, "Can we afford to do this program?" The really successful companies ask. "Can we afford not to do this program?"

A friend of mine did an excellent job of taking care of a customer. The client moved to a new company as the Chief Executive. He called in my friend to review his marketing program. He then told him that he was going to ask his marketing director to join them and asked my friend, "What do you think she will say about your ideas?" Now think, why did he ask that question? My friend knew why. He immediately reframed the question to one of eliciting feedback vs. personal and gave him as accurate answer to fit his expectation.

"She'll give you the OLD SCHOOL point of view, the old ways of doing things that appear on the surface to have no risk because EVERYBODY has done them in the past." Answered my friend.

He was right on. A short time later the Marketing Director was dismissed and my friends business increased.

NOW this was a result of an exchange with an Enlightened Decision Maker, who had been enlightened earlier by my friend. The executive called in an outside expert who excelled at selling.

3.2 - Induction of Collaborative Cooperation

Between You and the Client

Confidence Pattern

FACE TO FACE WITH THE PROSPECT:

You: Do you have a person with whom you feel absolutely confident, with me it my doctor. I'm not sure who it is that you go to on a regular basis, a family practitioner, a dentist, or some professional that provides you service? I'm sure there is one in whom you have confidence; with me I have one that I naturally confide in, me that is.

Prospect: Sure

You: I go to one that, you know, where you get that feeling of trust me, I think it's a function of trust me, I get that warm connection of trust. Are you with me?

Prospect: (Head Nod)

Confidence Pattern

You: Now, I don't know if you will believe everything I'm saying. Yet, I think it's important to me at least for you to understand that I want to assist you to make a good decision with me so we can determine whether this is absolutely the best product for you or not. So just in the same way, you confide in someone, me it has to be someone, whom you trust. Now, with me, I look at this interaction the same way.

So as we go through this, and you're looking at the information, listening to me and getting a really, really good feel for this. Think about all the ways this can assist you, and hopefully you will imagine how this can be implemented and work within your organization.

So if you need clarification on anything, please just stop me and we can clear it up for you. And, it's OK if I ask you questions as we go through this, YES?

Induction of Collaborative Cooperation

Between You and the Client

Relationship Pattern

FACE TO FACE WITH THE PROSPECT:

3.3 - Relationship Pattern and Eliminating Price and Competition

Prospect: I'm considering another vendor with better pricing.

You: Look, I'm not going to be the cheapest guy in town. Cheaper is not always better. I always ask a someone to look at the level of service and quality they expect in the final product. Now with me, selecting someone with whom you plan to form a business relationship is similar to, of course this is my notion, to the process you went through in selecting your family doctor. Have you ever had, or perhaps you have, a favorite physician or some other person that you have that connection with?

Prospect: Yeah

You: Well, if you went to their office and they decided you needed some blood work for whatever reason. You wouldn't even try to think to yourself "Well I don't know if this is the right thing." You, for the most part, you trust them and accept what they are saying and recommending based on the relationship you have with them. Wouldn't you?

Prospect: Yeah

You: You wouldn't even consider thinking to yourself "I bet there are about 50 other physicians who are closer to my home than this Doc and I bet they can even do my blood work for the same price or even less." Because let's face it, if a doctor is going to do blood work, it's a pretty standard procedure. We can agree the price is going to most likely be around the same price. 50, 60, maybe 70 dollars. Right?

Prospect: Yeah

You: The point (point finger in air) I am getting at is that there are probably some Docs that are closer to you, who can do the very same work for less money than your personal Doc. Yet you drive out of your way and probably spend a little more money. Why? Because of the personal relationship that you have with them, you trust them, you respect them, you probably even, like me, enjoy being around your own Doc. By now, I think you can realize I would like to have a personal relationship. With me, I hope you realize that you can call on me any time, me or my firm.

(Joke: even for blood work.)

3.4 - Combine and Package Client Information

Interweaving in Your Product and / or Service

Visual Pattern

FACE TO FACE WITH THE PROSPECT:

You: As you begin to focus up on this concept and pull it up closer, make it bigger and brighter, I think it will allow you to have a whole new view on how your business can operate even better; because with this product, it will allow you to have complete certainty knowing that you can have (Benefit) with the (product)

Move immediately into random sales stories with embedded commands moving toward buying, implementing, using, getting results.

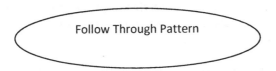

Follow Through Pattern

The absolutely best way to get referrals is to ASK FOR THEM. If you have a problem asking, YOU HAVE A PROBLEM.

Recently, the president of a Fortune 500 company had a crisis on his hands. A special situation came up where he needed blazingly fast response to connect up a bunch of people at the same time. No one on has staff could assist or had knowledge of even where to go on such short notice. All their sources failed. However, one vice president stepped forward and said, "Sir, you need to call Andy and Andy

Corporation (not his real name or corporation here, of course, this is an example as real as it may be). Now, Andy had never before performed such a service, who knows if the vice president knew this or not. What the vice president did know was that Andy was extremely knowledgeable and resourceful. He also knew that Andy had saved his butt on more than one occasion and would do the same for the president. Notice, he did not tell the president that he himself would take care of it. He knew he would get the recognition when Andy came through.

Andy, as you might have expected by now, delivered on time just as usual for him.

FACE TO FACE WITH THE **PROSPECT:**

You: A Customer who decided that this is the best product for them recently told a peer of mine, and I realize that it sounds funny; but, they said that after using this product that they had the same feeling that they had after they learned how to ride a bike or tie their shoe strings. In that, before they started, it seemed that back then learning those skills was an incredible accomplishment at that time, yet it's like you knew you were going to do this, that it has to be done, and maybe you were frustrated or scared learning how to do it but now it's an unconscious response.

And really learning to ride a bike or tie your shoes, back then, wasn't an option, it was something that you are going to do, no matter what, you're going to follow through with this because, heck, everybody else was doing it and now, this Customer said, heck I don't know how we ran our business without this product

Deciding to use this product is an unconscious response, a feeling of knowing it was right, this Customer said, because we are going to do this in one form or another, we might as well do it right with this product.

Combine and Package Client Information

Interweaving in Your Product and / or Service

Follow Through Pattern

Version for Visuals – moves quicker than the previous

FACE TO FACE WITH THE PROSPECT:

<YOU NOD YOUR HEAD – PROSPECT NODS>

You: A Prospect told a peer of mine that deciding to use (the product) is an unconscious response just like tying your shoes.

And I think that is true in that deciding to use (the product) is a natural, unconscious response because if your already need (the product) and you want it, obviously you're going to buy it because it just makes logical sense.

Now, I can't say you'll forget about all your concerns and suddenly realize that you need to buy it; yet, I believe that as I provide you the information you need in order to make a good decision. You will then feel good buying it.

Follow Through Pattern II

FACE TO FACE WITH THE PROSPECT:

<YOU NOD YOUR HEAD – PROSPECT NODS>

You: Now, obviously you're not going to unconsciously decide to buy this product without looking at all of the facts and letting yourself come to a logical decision that this is something you want to do, or something you need to do, or whether it's the right thing for you.

That's a fair assumption (nod)

COMBINE AND PACKAGE CLIENT INFORMATION
Interweaving in Your Product and / or Service

Future Pace Pattern I

FACE TO FACE WITH THE PROSPECT:

You: Just suppose it's a year from now and today, now you made the decision to go ahead with this now. Imagine that you are incredibly happy with this decision because you have achieved some amazing results. You're now *(Prospect Solution: work less, spend more time with family, activity)*, because of this product and your boss is really pleased with how well things have gone because of your decision to go with this and he has given you that appropriate recognition. What was it that I said, or you thought, that made you decide now to go ahead with this?

Message Pattern

FACE TO FACE WITH THE PROSPECT:
You:

Now, I am not suggesting that you will agree with everything you heard me say today; and entirely incorporate that information into your decision making strategy for making a good decision to go ahead with this now. I am suggesting, however, that you continue to think about this in an open-minded manner as to what is going to be explained here now. So that while I speak, you will begin to understand the validity of this information, not only will you agree with me all the way inside, yet you will act on any agreement and you will utilize it to really send a message. As it is sent you will start to feel complete. And your ability to rapidly decide to do this will allow you to realize this is the right thing to do.

3.5 - TURN CLIENT IN TO A SALES REPRESENTATIVE FOR YOU

Pride Pattern

FACE TO FACE WITH THE PROSPECT AFTER THEY DECIDE ON YOUR PRODUCT OR SERVICE OR IN A GROUP PRESENTATION:

You: Pride is really important in being able to endorse a product or service and even an organization; and it's similar to a friend of mine who's a surgeon. Out of the blue one day he asked me do you know why I am so excited about what I do? Do you know why I feel enthusiastic and feel proud with what I do? I think I gave him a confused look and just automatically asked "Why?". (or pace the Client's look)

He said, " last Saturday I was in a bookstore and I saw this couple with their two kids." I interrupted my doctor friend and asked, "What are you talking about? What does this have to do with feeling pride with what you do, enthusiasm and excitement?"

He said, "nine weeks ago I had that young man in surgery. Before surgery, I walked out of the operating room and fully explained the situation to the young woman. When I was walking through that bookstore and I saw him there with his family, I realized that by my professional skill, he was alive; I have such a wonderful feeling of pride." You see my friend made a decision a long time ago to assist people because he watched his father die of cancer and stood by helpless and he swore he would never let that happen ever again.

I am proud of your decision to go with this product and as you have that feel of pride to the point where you become so excited you naturally find yourself talking about this to everyone. You know the way a new father talks about his children. I believe it's similar to that in, that it's the type of decision and product that you can have a pride in, understanding this is the best decision.

Turn Client in to a Sales Representative for YOU

Gift Pattern

HOW TO GET A CONSISTENT PROSPECT TO SEND YOU REFERRALS:

This pattern is based on a symbolic gift and tying it to a symbol the person will use.

"John, I've been checking my records and I noticed that we've been doing business together for more than twelve months. You know, I get calls out of the blue from people who are in businesses similar to yours, and they ask me to come in and present what I have. My secretary and I almost always think to ask how they happened to call me. I have to believe that they are calling because good clients like you, have mentioned me in the course of conversation."

THEN YOU TAKE OUT SOME SYMBOL THAT WILL BE MEANINGFUL TO JOHN. IT CAN BE A SEMI-EXPENSIVE HIGH-QUALITY WRITING INSTRUMENT, A LEATHER PORTFOLIO, OR ANY GIFT THAT SPECIFICALLY RELATES TO JOHN'S NEEDS OR PREDISPOSITIONS.

"John, what I want to do is thank you for all the times you've recommended me to your friends. And I'd like to give you this small token of my appreciation for all the assistance you've been to me in the past, and for all the recommendations I've not stopped to thank you for till now, Bill."

Shake his hand, give him the gift and say,

"Thanks   (Client's   name).   Thanks   for   your recommendations."

3.6 - Sign Contract / Take Money / Get Purchase Order

Finish Pattern

FACE TO FACE WITH THE **PROSPECT:**

This pattern is based on future pacing, and allowing the Prospect to act out his/her own defense of his/her decision

You: I believe that you have made a really good decision to go ahead and buy this product, and I think that you would strongly feel the same as I do. Yet, I see this all the time when someone makes a really good decision, they realize it's the best thing for them, it's the right thing for them to do, they want, and they need. And someone comes along, and this someone doesn't mean any harm, it's just that they're trying to make you feel stupid or inadequate or they're jealous, who know and they're going to say to you, "Well do you really think we need it", "It costs too much" or anything that would cause you to question something that you know is true and right. You with me?

Prospect: Yeah

You: I'm curious, I know how I would respond, but how would you respond to someone who isn't as informed as you about this product, who is just trying to make you feel stupid in attempting to tell you this isn't the best thing for you?

Chapter 4 - Definition of NLP

Nuero

The nervous system (the mind), through which your experience is one processed via your five senses:

Visual
Auditory
Kinesthetic
Olfactory
Gustatory

Linguistic

Language and other non-verbal communication systems through which our neural representations are coded, ordered and given meaning. Which includes:

Pictures
Sounds
Feelings
Tastes
Smells
Words including self-talk

Programming

The ability to discover and utilize the programs that we run (our communication to ourselves and others) in our neurological systems to achieve our specific and desired outcomes.

Chapter 5 - Neurological Processes

External Event

This Course

Language   Decision   Memories

Filters

Hearing

Main Filters
Delete
Distort

Seeing

Tasting

Generalize

Feeling

LANGUAGE

Smelling

Decisions

Internal

Memories

STATE

BEHAVIOR

PHYSIOLOGY

5.1 – How the Brain WORKS

There are four characteristics of the brain which are critical to your understanding and; hence, execution of the knowledge herein contained.

First: The brain must answer questions, not just any question. It must answer ALL Questions. That does not mean that the mouth will utter a sound. The brain may not cause a verbal or visual response. Yet it still must answer the question. In fact the brain may provide a verbal response that is a LIE. I like to ask this one question for fun and to demonstrate. I ask, "How long have you been a closet homosexual?" The answer may be "never" or some other answers without a verbal or visual change of expression. The point to remember is that the ultimate response you get, that being a sale, is directly dependent on the questions you ask. How long have you been looking for a book like this and are just delighted at the prospect now of the future?

How many vendors have you dealt with that you felt just did not give you the service that you or any other company deserves?

Second: The brain is always looking for patterns. Patterns of what is poison in the way of animals and possible foods. Patterns of GOOD behavior and BAD behavior to provide a moral compass. Patterns of everything to determine what works and what does not. This pattern recognition ability is absolutely critical to keeping you alive. The brain is CONSANTLY looking for new patterns as this ability is ultimately responsible to the continuing existence of the human race. It is comparing everything you sense with the stored memories, the vast majority of which are unaware to the CONSCIIOUS MIND.

Think about it for a second. Laughter at a joke is part of this process. The comedian or person tells the set up and the brain compares this to a stored pattern. WHEN the punch line comes, THEN the brain learns that there is a new and different ending possible. It is happy because it just learned a new pattern.

Little Miss Muffet, sat on her tuffett eating her curds and whey, when along came a spider and sat down beside her and said:

What do you have in the bowl, WITCH?

Third: As part of the memory and pattern recognition mechanisms, the brain works in metaphors. These are high level generalizations that the brain uses to efficiently store images, patterns and descriptions. IT IS JUST LIKE is the easiest and most popular way to create a new metaphor. NOTICE: READING THIS BOOK IS JUST LIKE READING THE BIBLE WITH ITS NUGGETS OF WISDOM AND TRUTH ON VERY PAGE.

Fourth: In order to efficiently store everything you experience in life the brain use what I call a reference frame. You will make great use of this when Chunking Up or Down. Basically, as you are experiencing life, the brain is constantly comparing the experience both the similarity to previous experiences and the relevance of that experience to the ultimate safety structure it has also stored.

Let me briefly explain how a Television Signal Transmission works. You may have seen the old flip pictures where a series of still pictures are put in order and flipped with the thumb and the scene seems to be moving. In television a similar process is taking place. A REFERENCE image is sent and a fraction of a second later another image is ready to be sent. However, in digital television the second image is not sent. The second image is compared to the Reference image and ONLY the difference is sent or transmitted. Hence, only a very small amount of data is required to be stored or transmitted. This is why so much can be put on a DVD for example. As long as the background does not change very often the process is very efficient. The brain works the same way. Most of your experiences are very similar to those you have already had, thus most of the time they are overlaid with already stored experiences. The key point here is the use of a reference frame. When an experience occurs that is SUFFICENTLY different from those previously stored, then a new reference frame is created. This is the KEY understand in all Memory Enhancing courses.

I explicitly tell people, "I am the only person you will EVER meet with a first name YATES." I have just created a new reference frame. In our workshops, one of the exercises we use follows. We ask each person to stand up and introduce themselves in a unique way thu, creating a reference frame. The participants then give a thumbs up or down on the INTRODUCTION. Each person must continue until the group gives a great majority of thumbs up. On one occasion a young man stood up and said. "My name is Dan. I sell Mary Kay products and I am not wearing any underwear." He immediately got a unanimous thumb up.

When looking at these four attributes of the brain, keep in mind that the conscious mind is only aware of 2000 or so bits of information per second. The subconscious mind processes about 4,000,000,000 per second. YES, that is FOUR BILLION per second. You can now see why the subconscious is so important and why rapport within yourself and with your audience whether it be a single person one on one or an audience of thousands or millions is critical.

In other words, NLP can be how to use [1] the language of the mind to consistently achieve our specific desired outcomes.

NLP can be an attitude: It's an attitude of curiosity and wanton experimentation.

NLP can be a Methodology: A methodology of modeling and continual exploration.

NLP can leave a trail of techniques or patterns.

You will also become a behaviorist. Behavior is simply a function of the programming, values, beliefs, needs and habits any person has and it follows a feeling they have.

Before you can influence others you must first be able to influence yourself.

Remember, achieving success is an inside job. Motivation comes from inside your head. If it comes from outside your body then it is temporary and uncontrollable. In other words, you are a victim, a victim of circumstances, victim of genetics, and victim of society. You are not taking any responsibility for things that happen in your life.

5.2 - States, Physiology, Internal Representations

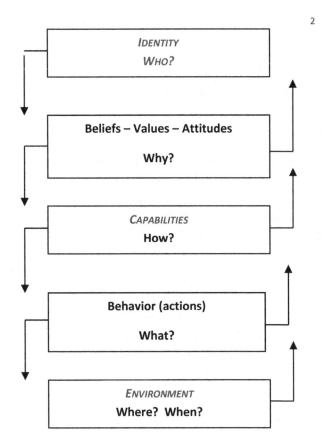

Values, beliefs and attitudes are the internal propulsion systems which drive the best persuaders and make them effective.

Remember, "God may forgive your sins but your nervous system won't?"

Programming	**>**	**Beliefs**
Beliefs	**>**	**Values**
Values	**>**	**Attitudes**
Attitudes	**>**	**Feelings**
Feelings	**>**	**Behavior (actions)**
Behavior (actions)	**>**	**Results**

5.3 - The Seven Words That Control Everything

A whole book could be written on these seven words and I may do so in the future. They are Why, How, Don't, Try, Can't, Yet and Up Until Now.

WHY is a word which causes you to rationalize. The brain answers the question by regurgitating what is already in the brain to justify the question. Why did you fail? Why did you succeed? Why did you not close and lock it last night?

In the live workshops, I asked a question of one of the participants. "What was it you wanted to do or wanted to be as a kid that just never happened?" I usually give an example of playing a sport or playing a musical instrument. It can be anything. Once this is established, I ask, "WHY did you not learn to play the piano?"

NO MATTER what answer they give, I ask, "Why didn't you do that?" or "Why did you let that stop you?"

Keep asking a WHY question no matter each successive answer. You will soon find the person in a loop giving you the same answer they gave you to begin the exercise. This type of circulatory rationalization keeps you stuck. You may find the answers are two or three deep; or they may be as many as eight or ten deep.

If you want to have some fun with your therapist, then just start asking them why questions.

HOW is a solution word. The brain will answer questions with how by searching both sides of the brain for connections and relationships. How could you have learned to play the piano? You can follow up with another how question.

You will notice that the answers to WHY questions are usually forthcoming very quickly because the answer is already stored in the brain as an answer or rationalization. The response to the HOW questions are usually much slower as the brain has to search and generate or create a solution.

You generally want to use WHY to reinforce a statement or belief. For example, why did you stay with our company for so many years?

You generally want to use HOW to move to a solution. For example, how can we resolve our differences? How would you see yourself making the decision to change companies?

DON'T is a very interesting word as the brain has to go through a special process to execute the word. The mind must think of what not to think. If I say now "Don't think of an orange" what comes to your mind. You have to think about what not to think about in order to not think about it; otherwise, you would not know what not to think about. GET IT. Some say that using the **_"don't"_** is just reverse psychology. It may be that AND it is much more. Typically put what you want them to do behind the "Don't". Don't think about all the ways you can use this now that you fully understand it.

TRY is the cousin of HOPE and denotes FAILURE. Remember as Yoda said, "There is no TRY there is ONLY DO." Again, learn how you use it and detect it in the language of others.

How many times has a friend or someone said to you, "I will try to be there?" Did they ever show up? Do you ever show up when you say you will TRY?

There is a place to use TRY for positive results. If a potential client for example who says, "I just want to get another bid and maybe get a better deal." You can simply say, "You can TRY."

CAN'T is a curse. Too many people today have heard the word "can't" too many times; or so often that they accept it. Look at what "can't" really means. It means that you currently are not able to do it; and you have never been able to do it, and you will never be able to do it. This is true no matter what IT is. There is no time element in "can't." So the net effect of saying "I can't" or believing without question "You can't" is the same as putting a curse on yourself or reinforcing a curse that you have already accepted.

It is like the elephant memory. He never forgets. You chain a baby elephant to a metal rod in the ground and he cannot escape. As he grows and remembers that he can't, then he does not even attempt to pull away.

One year while coaching a U12 Girls soccer team, we had a new player join the team. I asked her what position she played. She told me goalie; and proceeded to explain to me that she has been playing goalie for the past 4 years. She had gone to goalie school because her previous coach had told her four years earlier that she was too fat, could not run and the only position she could play was goalie. Baby Fat strikes again. She was not fat at 12 and she could run. After warm ups in the first practice, I assigned positions for the day. I told her to get in Midfield. She promptly announced she can't play midfield because she could not run.

I stopped practice and called the team closer. I looked at her and said, "Say that again."

She said, "Say what?"

I said your last comment about playing midfield. She repeated, "I can't play midfield...." I interrupted her, held out both hands palms up suggesting that she slap them and said, "Say that again and put the words "Up Until Now" after them."

I shook my hands indicating for her to take action. She slapped my hands hard and said, "I can't play midfield UP UNTIL NEVER."

At the end of the season she was chosen as an ALL STAR MIDFIELDER. When I presented the award and league championship trophy to her she asked, "Coach, should I go out for Goalie or Midfielder next year at school?" I answered, "Just go out for soccer player." The next fall there were about 80 girls who went out for the middle school team (grades 6, 7 and 8). She was one of three 6th graders to make the 22 player roster and started every game as midfielder or goalie.

UP UNTIL NOW is a modal operator of possibility. It lifts the time restriction from the CAN'T. Anything becomes possible from this point onward.

YET accomplishes the same as Up Until Now.

Chapter 6 - Beliefs, Values and Attitudes

A belief does not require something to be true. A belief only requires us to believe that something is true. Which means that most of what reality is to each of us is based on what we have come to believe – whether it's true or not is really our own opinion. The belief that we have about anything is so powerful that it can even make something appear to be something completely and totally different than it really is.

6.1 - *Beliefs*

Anything worth doing is worth doing. [3]

 Comparison and Contrast

 Anything worth doing is worth doing (Badly or Right).

 If at first you don't succeed then (Quit or try, try again).

There is no **_TRY_**. There is only **_DO_**.

If at first you don't succeed then look at what you did and DO something different next time.

I am responsible for my own outcomes. [3]

 Comparison and Contrast

 Others are responsible for my good and bad fortune.

 I am simply a victim of circumstances. (Bad or Good)

Work is a magnificent adventure.

 Comparison and Contrast

 Work is something we must tolerate until vacation.

 A job is something you must do to pay the bills. Or as one person put it once, JOB is Just Over Broke

In every adversity are hidden seeds of victory / opportunity. [3]

Comparison and Contrast

Adversity is nature's signal that you are about to lose.

Things don't get better by accident; things get better by appropriate [3] action.

Comparison and Contrast

You are either lucky or you are not lucky.

Some are born with it and some are not born with it.

Luck is when preparation meets opportunity. Are you prepared and looking for opportunity?

If I give others what they want and need, then they will give me what I want [3] and need, or "As ye sow so shall ye reap," or "What goes around comes around."

Comparison and Contrast

Only when somebody starts giving me what I want and

Need will I assist them too.

The Universe Will Provide

Commitment is the key to excellence 3

Comparison and Contrast

Commitment limits me too much.

The MORE committed you are the more GOOD things seem.

The LESS committed you are to something the MORE difficult things seem.

6.2 - Values

Long Term Thinking [4]

"In Search of Excellence" studied businesses such as Disney, McDonald's and Coca-a-Cola.   Each is built on a foundation of quality service, cleanliness and value; all long term attributes which lead to Customer satisfaction; which lead to referrals and repeat business.

As a current example, in discussions with a major client he said, "You know in our previous version of this product we had a real manageability problem.   As a matter of fact you really shouldn't buy any new (Initial Release) of any product.   You should wait until their 3rd or 4th release."   This statement was intended to be included in a marketing piece including a video.   A normal response upon seeing and hearing this would be to ignore it.   Our guy simply asked a question, "Is this the message you want to send to your end customers?   I ask this because I'm looking out for your best interest."   The customer revised the promotion piece with the statement deleted.

Positively Stated Outcomes [4]

All sentences need to be presupposed in the direction towards positive outcome for all.   You do this by concentrating on what everyone wants, while completely forgetting about what you don't want.

Clear Evidence Procedures [4]

You need to have a clear, concise game plan with each action quantified and dated.   A desire is not a goal until you attach a date to it and can measure it.   Then forget it, a watched pot never boils.   Focus on the processes.   Enjoy the journey.

Integrity is Congruency [4]

Integrity involves enough about other people to learn and understand their outcomes, goals and objectives before influencing them into assisting you achieve your goals, outcomes and objectives.   There must be alignment of both parties.

(See congruency in Extra Verbal Language Non-Verbal Language Section)

Values

Information Gathering Skills [4]

You need to gather sensory-specific information (including their words and language) which will give you an absolute advantage in learning about needs and perception of reality of the person or persons in front of you.

6.3 - Attitudes

Challenge is where the fun is

Ferocious Overwhelming Motivation

You can Party with your problems

Challenge is an opportunity to learn

Curiosity and Unrestrained Experimentation

Complete Flexibility of Behavior

Ferocity

Overwhelming Tenacious Resolve

You can sell anyone anything

No Hesitation – Direct Spontaneity

Life is good

You can motivate anybody

There is always a solution

You are dynamic

You can persuade anybody

You can create more at any moment in time

You can do anything

BLIND, UTTER OVERWHELMING TENACITY, FEROCIOUS RESOLVE AND INVINCIBILITY!!

• If what you're doing is not working, it is indicative of your lack of flexibility of behavior; it's not the prospect's fault, it's you, the operator's fault.   So if what you are doing is not working, do something else.   If what you're doing isn't working, it's an indication you are doing something ineffective for that situation.

• When something doesn't work the reason isn't that the person is a jerk.   You now have the unprecedented opportunity to learn something new.   After something is working so well, get someone else to do it.

• Look at every prospect as if it is a form of play, fun and curiosity. You should say to yourself, "Let the games begin." Remember: there is a difference between being thorough and playful versus being stupid and out of control.

• You need to be able to laugh at your problems and things that bother you. It's the first step in overcoming personal challenges. When you do have a personal challenge, difficulty or hesitation, say "Ahhh, Since I know I may not succeed, I can relax and just have fun, take action, learn and do new things.

• Thrill is the state which will allow you to do something new and different.

• You need to have an utter expectancy of success – not that you need to win each interaction as an end to feeling success – but just being able to learn something new about behavior is a thrilling success in itself.

Chapter 7 - Prerequisites

Tailor your presentations to your prospect's individual buying strategy. In order to tailor your presentation, you must understand what they need on many levels before influencing them to make a purchase decision.   And in doing so, you need to respond to their varied communication and thinking patterns.

Influence is based on your ability to first establish strong consistent rapport in the direction of your desired outcome.

Remember that there are two types of Persuaders. The Quantum Seller and one who is prerecorded with a canned presentation. Since you are a Quantum Seller, you need to qualify your client or audience or whomever you are persuading. Before you even begin the process of persuading and moving toward your outcome, you need to ask yourself:

- "How can I find out if this individual NEEDS what I have?" and

- "Is this the RIGHT THING for them?"

As for as finding qualified prospects, they are everywhere. You simply need to build a device from within you that will allow you to continually find qualified prospects. In other words; you need to know how and where to look for prospects.

Three foundational pieces in the persuasion process:

FIRST   Know yourself and know what you need to learn (i.e., technology, skill)

You need to have flexibility of behavior and you need to be able to look at all challenges as fun, and as an opportunity to learn something new.

SECOND Decisions are always being made and changed.

THIRD   Commitment = referral.

Decision without commitment = may mean sale with problems which includes no referral.

Persuasion is assisting someone make a decision. The final outcome of the ultimate persuasion process is a decision with commitment. When you have an individual with a happy decision connected to a satisfied commitment, he/she will then refer others to you.

Chapter 8 - Rapport and Pacing

8.1 Introduction

The single best way to establish rapport is to ASSUME RAPPORT. Put yourself in their shoes. If I were the owner, what would I do?

You don't need to establish rapport all the time, it may already be there. Although the following are effective techniques, they may be cumbersome and unnecessary.

Nevertheless, rapport is a critical ingredient in any persuasion process. If you focus on building rapport by becoming as much like the other person as possible – eliminating as many differences as possible, you may find it time consuming and actually anti-productive.

The conscious mind enables you to shift your attention from one thing to another. Therefore, whatever you are focused on and that you are aware of, is that part of you, which would be called your conscious mind.

The conscious mind is for the logical, that's why you do feature/benefit presentations. Yet during your presentation one of your outcomes should be the conscious programming of your client's unconscious mind.

The Unconscious mind is that part of you that contains your long-term memories. It is also in charge of all automatic behavior, that is, reflex action. In fact, the purpose of this training is to get you to be persuasive – automatically – by evaluating the way you automatically respond in persuasion situations, and then make instantaneous changes that will enhance the process.

> All Decisions are made by the unconscious/emotion.

Since the Unconscious is working all the time and is picking up all forms of communication (Verbal and Non-Verbal), this means you can be as overt with all the techniques as you want; just as long as it's the normal thing in the world for you and that everything is fine.

The definition of rapport is an unconscious connection. The whole idea of rapport is that likes attract each other and opposites repel. Pacing means getting in step with the prospect on as many levels as possible; getting into the ebb and flow of how that prospect thinks, acts, and processes data.

First, get into the rhythm of the client. Remember that people talk at the rate by which they process information. Mediocre persuaders tend to establish just a small amount of rapport and then move straight into influence strategies. By contrast, highly successful persuaders first build a strong rapport base, and then move into influence strategies.

8.2 - Emotional Rapport & Pacing

In emotional pacing we are trying to meet the client, or prospect, where he or she is emotionally at the moment of your first interaction.

The outcome is to develop rapport through pacing emotional feelings.

Some examples of emotional feelings which you need to sense:

Emotionally Down	Enthusiasm
Professional Demeanor	Depressed
Cold	Rushed
Disappointment	Delighted

If you do not pace your client you won't be able to establish enough rapport which is necessary to change his/her emotional direction. If you reject, contradict, minimize, or negate your clients emotional feelings directly or indirectly, you force your client to either defend his or her feelings or mentally dismiss you.

By using this strategy, emotional pacing allows you to step into the other person's reality. When you are in his or her world, only then can you see, feel and hear things from the client's perspective. You need to match the client's needs and predispositions. Consequently, the client will more readily accept your reality and only then move with increased ease toward your outcome.

8.3 - Agreement in Rapport & Pacing [5]

This type of rapport and pacing is based on getting the prospect in a yes mode. Remember that rhetorical questions are very, very, very powerful.

For example: Do you want to enjoy life more?

You do want to feel wonderful for a long time? Don't you?

> You want to be able to make a good decision, so you can come to a realization that this is absolutely the right thing for you?

Note: When you tell a person seven relevant things that he/she accepts as true, feels confident about or believes, the eighth thing you say will often be accepted without question.

In order to avoid coming across as contrived, pay special attention to personal philosophies regarding:

• Cost	• Values	• Trust
• Problems	• Opportunities	• Human Nature
• Risk Taking		

_____% of Sales Are Made After the _____ Sales Call

- 48% of sales people will make only 1 call
- 25% of sales people will make only 2 calls
- 12% of sales people will make only 3 calls
- 5% of sales people will make only 4 calls
- 10% of sales people will make only 5 calls or more

8.4 - Posture or Physiology Rapport & Pacing

Posture or Physiology pacing can be thought of as body language pacing. Posture rapport is the degree with which you are in physical harmony with that person and much of posture rapport is done from the chin up. There are many examples let's

list a few: Eye Movement, Eye Brow Movement, Head Movement, Smile, Touching Head with Hand.

The key is to be covert and to simultaneously pattern his/her movement.

There are three main ways to pace a person's behavior non-verbally.

1. Mirroring = It looks like they are looking in a mirror

2. Cross Over = Pacing with a different part of your body altogether

3. Matching = Opposite of a mirror

You can match:

Whole Body   Match/Mirror the other person's stance or overall position

Part Body	Match/mirror any consistent behavioral shrugs, gestures, head nods, or any other types of shifts in their behavior.
Half Body	Match/mirror upper or lower portion of other person's body.
Breathing	Match depth and/or speed. Breathing is one of the most powerful forms of non-verbal pacing.

How much should you match/mirror?

Somewhere around 50 to 80 percent of the movement will be effective – especially facial expression, shoulder posture, eye contact, sitting position and head nods.

Note: Problems can arise when we start interpreting body language, because you never really know what certain body posture and/or positions really mean.

8.5 - Language or Verbal Rapport & Pacing

Language pacing has two major components. One is patterning and the other is form. Patterning includes representational system codes and neurological context patterning. Form includes organizational and professional buzzwords which are also known as key words and/or trigger words.

Pacing words can be an extremely powerful rapport builder. Or, if not done correctly, it can be an extremely powerful rapport breaker.

8.5.1 - Representational Systems

All of an individual's ongoing experience must be comprised of some combination of each of his senses or "representational systems." Each person uses his/her sense of TASTE, TOUCH, HEARING, SEEING, AND SMELL to create his/her model of the world.

Due to the influences in the personal backgrounds of individuals, and the environments in which they develop their representational systems, there are tendencies for many people to develop or emphasize the information processing capabilities of one of their representational systems to a greater degree than others.

An auditory oriented person is one who prefers perceiving with his/her ears and who depends on the spoken word for the information which is decisive in his/her behavior.

A visually oriented person primarily uses his/her eyes to perceive the world around them, and he/she uses visual images in remembering and in thinking.

A kinesthetically oriented person is one who feels his/her way through his/her experiences.   Both external and internal stimuli are sorted through the feelings and these determine his/her decisions.

The predominant representational system will usually become obvious when a person is in a stressful or emotional state.

Our representational system creates for us a FILTERED or BIASED model of reality. This reality is very TRUE AND REAL to us.

As information comes into our brain, it goes through our FILTER.

The reason that we call it our representational system is because these five senses represent reality to us inside our own heads. So we actually don't operate on "pure reality."

We operate on our PERCEPTION or MODEL of "reality" which is based on how we FILTERED that information to ourselves. In other words, how we used our five senses to take the information in and store it.

Our representation of reality comes in initially through our five senses and then goes through some filters.

Thus, what we have are individuals who are communicating with each other in type of CODE. If you can unlock this, they will believe you understand them. And in fact, you will be understanding them better than you can imagine.

When you match someone's way of coding information verbally by using words from the representational coding system that they're using at that time, they don't have to recode what you've said into the coding system that makes better sense to them.

There is one more coding system that we will use. That representational system is called POSITIONAL system. This system comes from the visual system and is very useful to learn.

The way to determine if a word is unspecified is to determine whether it can fit into more than one coding system. If it can then it is an unspecified word.

For example, let's demonstrate using the word UNDERSTAND:

Can you understand something you see? Sure. Can you understand something you hear? Sure. Can you understand something you feel? Sure. Because the word, understand, fits into more than one system, it can be classified as unspecified.

"**Predicates**" are words, such as verbs, adverbs and adjectives, which indicate actions or qualities as opposed to things. *This type of language is typically selected at an unconscious level* and thus reflects the underlying mental structure which produced them. Through their language, people will literally tell you which representational system they are employing to make sense of and organize their ongoing experience.

Whenever you mismatch predicates, it automatically produces distrust.

Beside each of the phrases below, write a (V) for visual, (A) for auditory, and a (K) for kinesthetic or (U) for unspecified, to indicate which rep system is presupposed by the phrase.

I see what you are saying

That doesn't look quite right

I hear you

I've got a good feeling about this

I need to get clear on this idea

Get a handle on this

That rings a bell

Unlimited potential

It sounds good to me

Think about it

Pleasing personality

He needs to get in touch

It's sort of hazy right now

It just suddenly clicked

I just go blank

I had to ask myself

A colorful example

We're up against a wall

Go with the flow

Networking

Listen to this

Branch out

A solid proposal

We need a new perspective

Cool

Tune into what they're

Trying to say

Tight situation

That casts some light on the subject

8.5.2 - Eye Movements

The direction and position to which an individual momentarily looks with his or her eyes when recalling information or answering a question corresponds to the representational system they are accessing.

During interaction, when a person often breaks eye contact, the eye movements indicate whether one is using pictures, words, or feelings in thinking and remembering. These eye movements are a class of behavior called "accessing cues."

Accessing cues are automatic **unconscious** eye movements which accompany a particular thought process indicating the accessing of one of the representational systems. These eye positions can also stimulate access to and support activity in a particular sensor system as well.

In the following diagram, the directions of the eyes are explained according to which representational system is being used:

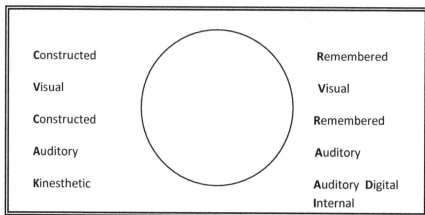

Constructed	Remembered
Visual	Visual
Constructed	Remembered
Auditory	Auditory
Kinesthetic	Auditory Digital
	Internal

8.5.3 - Visuals [6]

It is estimated that about 35% of the US population are Visuals. Their minds turn everything into pictures. Visuals have great memories. They can describe how things look in minute detail. They remember colors, shapes and forms. They also think in images when fantasizing about the future. Appearance is important for visually oriented people.

Note: A person maybe lying when asked a direct question and eyes shift up to the right or straight right, a sign that the person is creating images or words.

Visual Statements:

I see what you are saying.	I can picture that.
That doesn't look quite right.	It's pretty clear to me.
I need to get clear on this idea.	Looks good to me.
It's sort of hazy right now.	I just go blank.
We need a new perspective.	A colorful example.
That's a pretty bright idea.	Can you show it to me?
That casts some light on the subject.	

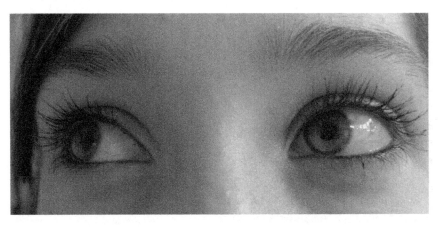

Right and Up with the eyes

Visual Construct (V^c) Images are constructed Where the prevailing hemisphere is visualizing pictures. Thinking about the future. Tension in shoulders Shallow breathing and in the chest

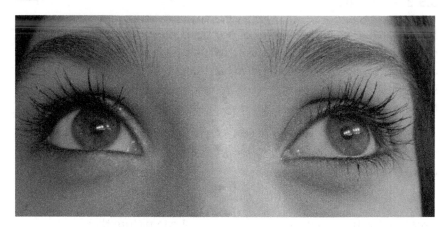

Left and Up with the eyes Visual Remembered (V^r). Images are Remembered or Reconstructed. Where the non-prevailing hemisphere is remembering pictures. Thinking about the past. Tension in shoulders Shallow breathing and in the chest

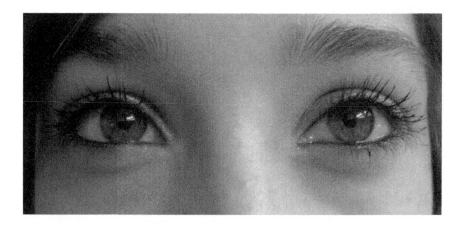

Straight Ahead / De-focused – Synthesizing thoughts – converting words and feelings into images

Tension in shoulders Shallow breathing in the chest

Visual Characteristics:

Visuals maintain good eye contact – voice high-pitched and fast – good with directions – good visual memory – they breathe high up in the chest – speak in rapid bursts – tend to be thinner in body build, and often dress better than others in their economic range

Visual Predicates:

An eyeful	Analyze	Angle
Appears	Aspect	Clear
Clear-cut	Notice	Notice
Bright	Clarity	Clue
Cognizant	Conspicuous	Demonstrate
Dim view	Discern	Dream
Examine	Eye to eye	lash
Focus	Foresee	Get an image
Glance	Hazy idea	Get a perspective
Hindsight	Horizon	Look
Make a scene	Mental image	Mental picture
Bird's-eye view	Mind's eye	Naked eye
Obscure	Observe	Obvious
Outlook	Outstanding	Paint a picture

Peep	Perception	Picture
Zoom in	Foggy	Glare
Perspective	Idea	Illusion
Illustrate	Image	In light of
In view of	Inspect	Recognize
Scrutinize	See	See red
See to it	Shortsighted	Show
Show-off	Sight	Sight for sore eyes
Sign	Sketchy	Photographic
Memory	Pinpoint	Pretty as a picture
Plain	Plainly see	Survey
Read	Stare	Diagram
Up-front	Vague	View
Vision	Watch	Well-defined
Envision	Perceive	Illustrate
Highlight	Prevue	Aim
Dark	Glow	Portray
Scan	Dull	Shine
Cloudy	Light	Reflect
Telltale sign	Hide	Brilliant
Oversight	Diagram	Blind
Tunnel vision	Visible	Horse of a different color

Staring off into space   Beyond a shadow of a doubt

8.5.4 - Auditory [7]

It is estimated that about 25% of the US population are Auditories. Auditories listen to the way you say things. Usually, they get more information from how you say something than they do from what you are saying. Auditories love the telephone. Often auditories say things they don't mean to say. They actually need to hear their words in order to understand what they're thinking. By then it's too late to stop. These people will touch their faces when they talk to you.

Auditory Statements:

That rings a bell   I hear you

It sounds good to me   Listen to this

It just suddenly clicked   I had to ask myself

All I ever get from you is static   Say did you hear the one about

Can you tell me more about it   Can you tell me how it works

Tune in to what they're trying to say

Don't take that tone with me young man

That idea has been rattling around in my head for a while

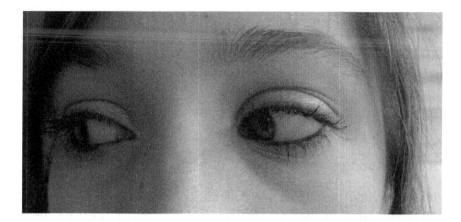

Right and Level with the eyes Auditory Construct (A^c) Sounds are constructed Where the prevailing hemisphere is creating words and sounds. Thinking about the future. Shoulders leaning back. Even breathing from the center of the chest

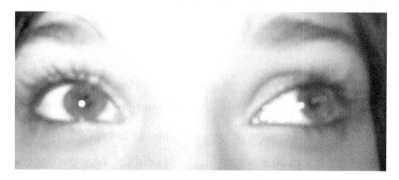

Left and Level with the eyes Auditory Remembered (A^r) Sounds are Remembered or Reconstructed. Similar to a tape recorder. Where the non-prevailing hemisphere is remembering sounds and words or even past verbal sequences. Thinking about the past. Shoulders thrown back Even breathing from the center of the chest

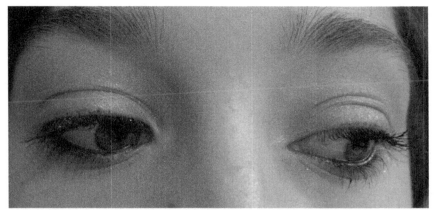

Left and Down with the eyes Auditory Internal Dialogue (A^i_d) Client is talking to themselves. Hand is touching face, or index finger tapping chin. Synthesizing thoughts – converting words to sounds. Shoulders even. Breathing slow with one deep breath

Auditory Characteristics:

They will speak in a lower tone, rhythmically, smooth and deliberately, conscious of every word. Their breathing is similar – slower and deeper than that of visuals. When auditories are looking down to the left, they are talking to themselves, so when you notice this, allow some time for their internal conversation to play itself out. If you continue talking, they won't hear you. Auditories will speak in an even and pleasant voice register, and occasionally you will hear them hum, whistle, or make clicking sound.

Auditory

Amplify	Articulate	Audible
Announce	Ask	Blabbermouth
Boisterous	Call	Clear as a bell
Clearly expressed	Comment on	Communicate
Describe in detail	Discuss	Dissonant
Divulge	Earful	Earshot
Give me your ear	Exclaim	Express yourself

Give an account of	Enunciate	Gossip
Grant an audience	Hear	Heard voices
Hidden message	Interview	Hush
Idle talk	Inform	Inquire
Hold your tongue	Invite	Keynote speaker
Loud and clear	Listen	Loud
Mention	Mutter	Noise
Oral	Outspoken	Overhear
Pay attention to	Power of speech	Proclaim
Pronounce	Purrs like a kitten	Quiet
Quoted	Rap session	Remark
Report	Rings a bell	Roar
Rumor	Scream	Screech
Shout	Shrill	Sound
Silence	Speak	Talk
Speechless	Squeal	State
Manner of speaking	Suggest	Tattletale
Tell	To tell the truth	Tone
Tongue-tied	Tune	Utter
Tuned in or tuned out	Voice	Unheard of

Voiced an opinion	Vocal	Utterly
Static	Accent	Resonate
Yell	Rasp	Sing
Babble	Whine	Tone
Boom	Chime	Snore
Music	Clatter	Aloud
Verbalize	Clang	Squawk
Debate	Shriek	Hiss
Well-informed	Within hearing range	Word for word

8.5.5 - Kinesthetic [8]

It is estimated that about 40% of the US population are kinesthetics. Kinesthetics gather information primarily from touch, emotions, gut instincts, and hunches. Kinesthetics are quick to pass judgment. Some kinesthetics have a hard time making eye contact because they are searching for a feeling. A kinesthetic is the type of person who will offer you a coffee, Coke, cookies or something else, always accept the offer, refusal leads to discomfort for a kinesthetic.

Kinesthetic Statements:

Get a handle on this
We're up against a wall
Let's touch base next week
Here is my feeling on that
I've got a good feeling about this project
Can you grasp what needs to be done?
Here's what I feel about what you just said

A solid proposal
That's a heavy problem
It rubs me the wrong way

She needs to get in touch with the flow of the sentiment

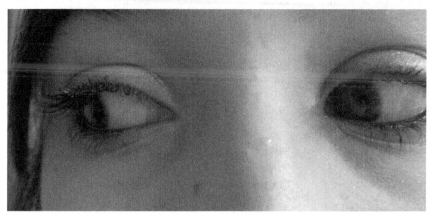

Right and Down with the eyes Kinesthetic Awareness (K). Synthesizing thoughts – converting words to feelings. Shoulders down. Deep abdominal breathing

Kinesthetic Characteristics:

Kinesthetics are people who talk with frequent pauses because they are grasping for a feeling. They tend to speak somewhat slow in a low and resonant voice and frequently touch their clothing or their bodies. Specifically, touching the mid-line. Loving to touch people and things is another characteristic of the kinesthetic. When you are talking with them across a desk, they are often playing with small objects; they seem to pick them up without thinking: pens, paper clips, erasers, pieces of paper. Touching gives them a feeling of contentedness. Kinesthetics tend to breathe fully and deeply, using gestures when speaking. People who have a muscular body build tend to be kinesthetic; in their latter years they have a tendency to be overweight. Kinesthetics are also sensitive to temperature changes. A kinesthetic is the one who speaks up first when hot or cold.

Kinesthetic

Active	Affected	All washed up
Bearable	Boils down to	Callous
Charge	Cold	Come to grips with
Comfortable	Concrete	Foundation
Control	Cool	Cutting
Depth	Effort	Embrace
Emotional	Experience	Fall apart
Feel	Firm	Floating
Flow	Flush	Forceful
Chip off the old block	Handle	Get a handle
Hang	Hand in hand	Hang in there
Get a load of	Know-how-this	Lay your cards
Get in touch with	On the table	Light-headed
Get the drift	Lukewarm	Lump
Get your goat	Moment of panic	Grasp
Grip	Motion	Grow
Move	Hard-headed	Hassle
Head on	Heated	Heated argument
Heavy	Hold	Hold it
Hold on	Hot-headed	Hunch
Hurt	Hustle	Intuition

Involve	Keep your shirt on	Muddled
Not following you	Panicky	Pressure
Pull some strings	Push	Respond
Rough	Rush	Seized
Sense	Sensitive	Sharp
Caress	Cuddle	Hug
Pat	Stroke	Shift
Slipped my mind	Shock	Snap
Smooth	Smooth operator	
Soft	Solid	Sore
Stand for	Start from scratch	Wear
Stiff upper lip	Stir	Stress
Structure	Stuffed shirt	Suffer
Support	Weary	Whipped
Swelling	Tap	Tension
Tied up	Tight	Tired
Too much hassle	Topsy-turvy	Touch
Underhanded	Unsettled	Warm

8.5.6 - Unspecified

Additionally, unspecified words are words that fit into any representational coding category. Listed below are a few from the Unspecified Category.

Logical	Organize	Express
Evaluate	Feedback	Explain
Ponder	Select	Rational
Cooperate	Interact	Teach
Reward	Plan	Relate
Change	Intuit	Give
Experience	Need	Want

The most powerful unspecified words which can cause trans-derivational searches are:

Think	**Aware**	**Experience**
Know	**Wonder**	**Notice**
Understand	**Sense**	**Learn**
Remember	**Believe**	**Consider**

Note: When in doubt, as to which representational system predicates to use; use predicate combinations and/or unspecified predicates.

CAN YOU SEE WHAT I'M TALKING ABOUT?

ARE YOU GETTING A GOOD FEEL FOR WHAT I AM

DESCRIBING TO YOU?

PICTURE WHAT I AM SAYING?

Note: A good confusion pattern is when you cross over representational systems that do not match. Such as:

CAN YOU FEEL WHAT I SEE?

HEAR WHAT I PICTURE?

CAN YOU SMELL WHAT I TASTE?

CAN YOU FEEL WHAT I HEAR?

8.6 - Buzz or Key Words [9]

Key words can be jargon or buzz words. Buzzwords are often cues to let the other know that you have read the latest article, the latest book, or

have talked to people knowledgeable about the industry to which you are selling. The importance of buzzwords is that buzzwords establish an identification of who is in tune and who is not.

Note: If someone does use a buzzword that you are not familiar with, stop and ask them to clarify.

For example, a computer programmer would use technical terms related to programming, such as bandwidth, hard-disk, Random Access Memory (R.A.M.), Read Only Memory (R.O.M.).

8.7 - Trigger Words

Trigger words carry emotional impact. Trigger words are the type of words that pop out at you because they're colorful or extreme in meaning.

For example:

If you're selling a house and your client says, "What I want is a house with an **incredible** view."

In this sentence, the word that carries the most emotional weight would be "incredible." Now that you have identified this word you can use the word incredible in a different context and whatever directional thought that precedes or follows the word "incredible" carries a lot more emotional neurological persuasion power.

For example: A Prospect said "In one word this system needs to be "r e e e e l i i i able"......

Now whenever you talk about your product use the exact word "r e e e e l i i i able!!"

8.8 - Parroting or Reflective Listening

Parroting or reflective listening is a form of active listening. This technique is simply repeating some of the exact same words in the same order and sequence, that your client uses, right back to your client. This technique allows your client trust you.

Never, Never, Never paraphrase someone else's thoughts. By changing one word you change their unconscious meaning. A person is unconsciously precise about what they say based on the way their unconscious organizes their representational systems and filters, etc.

When using this technique you need to be artful or you will offend the person. Used subtly, this is very powerful technique, especially when the other person is emotional about a topic.

Another great side benefit of this technique is that what you say back will reinforce that thought in the other persons' mind. Use it carefully, and you will automatically remain in the same representational system of the person you are matching.

What is even 10 times more powerful is picking up language structures from a person, that you want to influence, while they are talking to someone else. So while they are not consciously focused on you and speaking to someone else, you pick up AND take mental notes of their patterns. Then when they finally direct their conscious mind back to you and you repeat their linguistic patterns from a different context, while simultaneously move towards your outcome, you amplify unconscious agreement with persuasion power tenfold. (See the section on Context, Content, and Process)

Parroting or reflective listening deepens rapport three ways: It shows that you are paying attention; that you understand what the person is telling you; and that you care.

Remember: We all have different ideas of reality – ways in which we perceive the world – and we can only really trust people who see, hear and feel the word the same way we do.

8.9 - Voice, Tone and Tempo Rapport & Pacing

With your voice match: tonality, tempo (speed), volume (loudness), intensity, rhythm, inflections, and intonation patterns of your client.

From the aforementioned list, matching tempo and tonality are the two most important variables to consider when pacing verbally. Voice Tone and Tempo are critical, especially while doing phone work.

Remember, tempo is most important because people do not process information any faster or slower than at the rate at which they speak. As a professional communicator, it is your job to vary all components of your voice. (See Extra Verbal Language / Non-Verbal Language section specifically Intonation Patterns)

In hypnosis, voice tone and tempo are key elements. The concept is to just lower your voice and slow down the pace at which you are speaking; thus, slowing down a person's internal processes.

Here is an example that is fun and makes the strong and necessary point of just how important voice, tone and tempo are.

Take this sentence and say it numerous times and each time you say it, with emphasis on the underlined word.

You can do it all night long.

You can do it all night long.

You **CAN** do it all night long.

You can **DO** it all night long.

You can do **IT** all night long.

You can do it **ALL** night long.

You can do it all **NIGHT** long.

You can do it all night **LONG**.

In our work shop we have a person give one sentence written on a piece of paper to a different person. We then have them all come up to the front of the class and line up according the word emphasized in their sentence. They in turn read the sentences. The context has a lot to do with the meaning. Set the context as relationships or seduction and you get one set of meanings. Set the context as the ability to work long hours and you get another set of meanings.

No matter the context, you get a different meaning to the sentence depending on the word you emphasize.

In a casino on Paradise Island on night in the Bahamas, I asked two young ladies that were walking by the craps table if they would like to play a game. I explained that our young friend was about to have his turn throwing the dice and would they please stand behind him and whisper the sentence into his ear with each taking turns. He went into trance and held the dice for about 30 minutes. We all made a lot of money and gave each of the girls $50.00 each for their contribution. As a side note our friend lost the dice when the young ladies' attention was drawn away from him by two other young men on the corner of the table who heard the whispers and did not have their minds on craps. Do you understand?

8.10 - Values and Beliefs, Rapport and Pacing [10]

The primary outcome when pacing and building rapport is not to step on the other person's values and beliefs. The more highly valued the other person's beliefs or values are, the more important it is not to trounce on them. Since people are only interested in doing business with people who are like them, it is in your best interest to have some level of rapport based on values and beliefs.

When using values and beliefs pacing in building rapport, emphasize the points of agreement and deemphasize or ignore the points that are irrelevant to the agreement frame. Make sure that you don't compromise yourself when you pace values and beliefs. No matter what a person believes, there will always be something about that value or belief that you can feel comfortable in pacing, even if it is a tiny percent of the entire opinion or belief.

The best way to establish and maintain values and beliefs while pacing is to never take exception. Remember, you must focus on agreement and harmony.

8.11 - Cultural [11]

Cultural pacing and rapport is broad, yet refers specifically to internal corporate cultures of an organization. For example:

Dress Code: At one time if a man went to an interview for a job at E.D.S. and if that man was not wearing a pressed, white shirt he was never asked back for a second interview.

Sexual Connotations: In some organizations, if a man makes a statement such as "That's a gorgeous dress you are wearing." It can be perceived by some as a sexual harassment. A less harmful statement would be "That's an attractive outfit you have." For the most part be tasteful, sincere, honest and tactful; and mix that all together with good judgment. When you are in doubt, forget about doing it.

Protocols: In more traditional organizations there are procedures, as to whom you speak to first, who gets called by his/her first name, who you use Mr. or Mrs. with, whom you lunch with etc. etc.

Today with empowerment, some managers are delegating major decisions to administrators closer to the front line; even with that you must continue to focus your concentration to the higher levels of the organization when selling.

When offered a cup of coffee, soda, cookie, or any other food item, by all means graciously accept it.

8.12 - Content Rapport and Pacing

Content rapport and pacing is when you simply meet your client where they are, with references to the topic or subject they are interested in talking about, and you simply let yourself become engrossed in what they want to talk about by asking questions or adding truisms; and while doing this you can simply and naturally ease into your outcome.

For example:

Prospect: Let's get to the bottom-line

Rep: What's the important issue, to you, with this product?

Prospect: Accuracy.

Rep: What about accuracy, tell me about accuracy

Prospect: Well I did research in college and ......

The Prospect and the rep then went on and discussed all the issues that pertained to accuracy for over 15 minutes.

8.13 - Amplification of Rapport and Pacing [12]

Amplification is accomplished by:

Assisting your client focus in on how you can assist them achieve their goals.

Noticing reading material, pictures or hobbies but this type of amplification needs to be sincere and not stereotypical or mechanical. Note: This sometimes produces false rapport.

Wearing certain pins such as an American Flag or Rotary Pin.

REMEMBER: The main outcome and purpose of

Rapport and Pacing is to get the other person to

TRUST YOU.

Mirroring is an excellent way to find out if you and your client are connected. If you are both connected, the client will match your movements. If you do or say something that the client does not like, then miss-matching will occur.

Now we need to learn a couple of additional things that will make this more precise and predictable. It's called Pacing and Leading.

The definition of pacing is when you SAY or DO things that are verifiably true in a person's ongoing sensory experience.

The definition of leading is when you are doing something DIFFERENT than the other person is doing.

Thus, the test for rapport is when you lead by doing something different than the other person is doing and if he/she follows you within 1 – 5 seconds, then you have them.

Of course the quicker they respond the deeper your connection, the greater your rapport and the greater your persuasion power.

If they don't respond, then you go back to PACING.

When they follow your lead immediately, then you go into the state that you want them to be in, that will allow you to achieve your outcome, because they will follow your state.

Note: When leading someone into a state, focus on breathing and facial changes such as coloration and pore sizes.

PHYSICAL CHANGES always follows STATE CHANGES, which means you need to be a sensory acuity machine, a bio-feedback mechanism.

Chapter 9 - Sensory Acuity and Calibration

1.   Make sure you always have an outcome in mind when using these techniques. It makes your aim sharper and you won't fall prey to the rapport that you created.

2.   How do you break rapport?   Stop pacing them OR begin to mismatch.

3.   The deeper you want your rapport to be:

    A.   Pace more behavior, attitudes, beliefs, rep systems, etc.

B.   Make your movements at the same time they do. (lead up to this)

4.   To test for rapport – change your behavior.

If they follow, you're in rapport.

Remember the outcomes of Rapport and Matching are mutual acknowledgment, liking, respecting, accepting, understanding and

THE MOST IMPORTANT INGREDIENT
TRUST.

Chapter 10 - The Communication Success Formula:

1. _____

2. _____

3. _____

_____

4. _____

_____

_____

Chapter 11 - Content, Context, Process and Structure

This section corresponds with the "Collect and Gather Client Buying Criteria and Strategy" in the "Sale Cycle" Section.

Content is simply the main and overall abstract FACTS of conversation.

Context is the unconscious neurological form or patterning of the thoughts concerning a particular subject or topic. In the formation of a sentence, context is before and after the meaning within the sentence.

Process is the method by which an individual moves through an operation, usually involving steps in a certain sequence in order to produce a desired result or thought.

Structure / Syntax is the arrangement or interrelation of all the parts of a whole.

All influence, persuasion and meaning is CONTEXT, PROCESS, AND SYNTAX dependent.

Context, Process, Syntax and Structure are one of the most critical aspects of persuasion! Learn to think, talk and write in terms of context, process, syntax and structure, not content. By focusing in on only process you will see immediate and powerful increases in your personal persuasion ability. This section could also be called the "HOW People Think" section.

When you break apart language, and diagram the Context, Process and Structure, it is called strategy.

Strategy is a set of explicit mental and behavioral steps used to achieve a specific outcome. In persuasion, one of the most important aspects of a strategy is the representational systems used to carry out the specific steps.

Process is the direction, content is the method of travel and structure is your map or flight plan.

The questions to ask in order to elicit a buying strategy are important in unpacking a strategy. Yet the questions, if asked properly, do more than allow you, as the operator, to just gather information.

The goal in asking precise questions is to naturally or covertly facilitate the client to execute a trans-derivational search.

A **Trans-derivational Search** is the process of searching back through one's stored memories, mental representations and/or internal processes to find the reference experience from which a current behavior or response is being derived.

Evoking a trans-derivational search within the client causes them to relive/rehearse that experience and access the process/strategy that they use in their past to make similar decisions.

Just by asking the right question(s) to cause a trans-derivational search, you simultaneously evoke the associated emotions, which you are inquiring about. Unconsciously you are causing the client to anchor those associated feelings, emotions and processes to you, your service and/or product.

Anchoring is the process of associating an internal response with some external trigger (similar to Pavlovian conditioning) so that the response may be quickly and sometimes covertly reassessed.

An example of some questioning structures that can cause trans-derivational searches and will simultaneously give you process information are:

- "What caused. . ."

- "How did you decide to. . ."

- "What would lead you to. . ."

- "How did you determine that. . ."

- "How did you choose. . ."

- "What would convince you that. . ."

These questions will get you process information. The best way to uncover process-oriented information is to simply listen for it as the person you are persuading talks. They are continually giving you process information yet you need to know what to specifically look and listen for, and have the sensitivity and skill to gather the correct information.

The procedure that the client moves through within their mind, from start to finish is what you are to listen to. When you're learning how to listen for process it is critical to listen very very carefully, because everything taken in by your ears and eyes are clues to uncovering process.

You: "In selecting your last car, how did you determine it was the right car for you."

Prospect:

"HHMMM" – *pause* – "First, I looked around and determined what features I wanted. Then, I talked to four or five sales people at different dealerships and listed out all the possible models and corresponding options. This allowed me to get a smart feel for what would be best for me. I then figured out what would be the most economical and thought about it for a week because I didn't want to jump in too quickly."

Analyze the Prospect's response from two perspectives, first representational system codes and secondly, structure and process.

List the steps the person goes through on the next page. List the VAK codes the person utilized on an unconscious level and look at the process structures and procedures the person moves through in order to make a decision. Remember order, syntax and sequences are critical in allowing you to achieve your outcome with your client.

List the <u>V.A.K. Codes</u> on the left a person goes through in order to make a decision (in syntactical order). List the steps on the right that a person goes through on a global level to make a decision.

<u>Buying Criteria Sequence Codes</u>

1. _____   1. _____

2. _____   2. _____

3. _____   3. _____

4. _____   4. _____

You: Just for my edification, because I'm curious and because every organization has its own protocol and internal procedures, and I want to be convinced that we are doing the right thing for this organization. If we were to move on to the next step in order to find out as to whether this is the best decision for this organization to go with this product, what will you have to do to get the ball rolling internally; and the reason why I am asking is because by my becoming aware of this process, it allows me to do a better job with you and for you. (*pause*) Are you with me?

Client: That's a very good question. Let me see. Well, we would take a closer look to see if it fits in with our strategic direction and it would have to fit in tactically from an organizational standpoint. Then I would get my three in house experts to meet with you, my front-line vice-presidents, and of course you would have to sell them. And if everyone was in agreement after analyzing it and everyone felt secure, we would roll it out.

So I guess the next step would be for me to set up a time where you can meet my vice-presidents.

List the <u>V.A.K. Codes</u> on the left that a person goes through in order to make a decision (in syntactical order). List the steps on the right that a person goes through on a global level to make a decision.

<u>Buying Criteria Sequence Codes</u>

1. _____   1. _____

2. _____   2. _____

3. _____   3. _____

4. _____   4. _____

Chapter 12 - Extra Verbal Language and Non Verbal Language

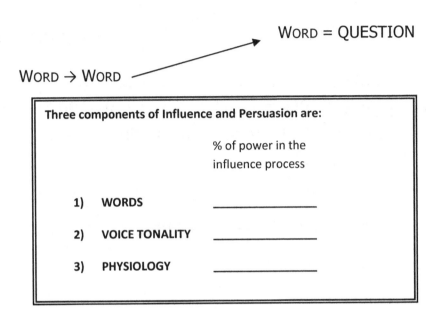

INTONATION PATTERN I

WORD → WORD

WORD = QUESTION

Three components of Influence and Persuasion are:

% of power in the influence process

1) WORDS   _____

2) VOICE TONALITY   _____

3) PHYSIOLOGY   _____

INTONATION PATTERN II

Word → Word   Word →   =   STATEMENT

"Natural speech does not consist of words alone. It consists of utterances – an uttering-forth of one's whole meaning with one's whole being – the understanding of which involves infinitely more than word recognition."

Dr. Oliver Sacks

INTONATION PATTERN III

WORD → WORD

WORD = COMMAND

Congruence – Is when all of a person's internal beliefs, strategies, and behaviors are fully in agreement, alignment and oriented toward securing a desired outcome.

CHAPTER 13 - PRESUPPOSITIONS

A PRESUPPOSITION IS SIMPLY THE LINGUISTIC EQUIVALENT OF AN ASSUMPTION. THE POWER OF A PRESUPPOSITION IS THAT IT GENERATES AN INTERNAL REPRESENTATION. WHEN YOU HAVE A PERSON GENERATING AND CREATING INTERNAL REPRESENTATIONS EITHER CONSCIOUSLY OR UNCONSCIOUSLY WHILE MOVING TOWARDS YOUR OUTCOME YOU WILL ACHIEVE THAT OUTCOME VERY QUICKLY.

When delivering a presupposition you must state everything in a direction towards your outcome and it must be delivered in a congruent manner. So while communicating you must concentrate on exactly what you want, NEVER CONSIDER WHAT YOU DON'T WANT, IN FACT JUST FORGET ABOUT WHAT YOU DON'T WANT.

Note: Remember presuppositions need to be grouped in three's.   (See Formal Structural Format of Embedded Command)

You will be incongruent if you go after an outcome that is what you should want versus what you really want, AND you know you are incongruent if you procrastinate while trying to achieve an outcome. Which means that your outcome must capture every fiber of your soul and being?

Example:

"If my sales rep knew how much I suffered, he wouldn't do that.   It's just not fair."

Presupposition 1:   _____

Presupposition 2:   _____

Presupposition 3:   _____

Presupposition 4:   _____

Presupposition 5:   _____

Example: "As you begin to think about all the benefits that you're learning from this course, do you think you will tell everyone you come in contact with how great it is?"

Presupposition 1:   _____

Presupposition 2:   _____

Presupposition 3:   _____

Presupposition 4:   _____

Presupposition 5:   _____

Presupposition 6:   _____

Chapter 14 – The 18 Most Influential Words [11]

These key words are utilized by television, radio, and print advertisers with enormous effectiveness. Some of these words are so effective, that even though companies overuse them, people still unconsciously respond to them positively. Advertisers have been light-years ahead of the rest of us in appreciating how certain words have greater psychological impact. They understand that words can motivate, bring back memories, and evoke deep feelings. Advertisers know how to use words to persuade, entice, cajole, entertain, and in the best of circumstances, educate. They have learned how words can make people look at things in totally new ways and perhaps try something they have never tried before.

1. Discover. A word that would generate interest, evokes a feeling of [11] opportunity, and suggests a better life. Remember that when you tell your clients that they will discover something, you will evoke the associated feeling to whatever you want them to discover.

2. Good. "As good as mother used to make"; "It's good for you"; "The Good Old Boys." Good is not a high-powered word, and that is the secret of its success. It evokes stability and security. If something is good for your clients, they will want to buy it. And by extension, if it's good, it's not bad. Everyone wants to be associated with what is good.

3. Money. Few people feel they have enough, and everybody wants more.

4. Easy. What everyone wants is more simplicity and the ability to do things more easily. If your product can make something easier for would-be purchasers, they will be more apt to buy it.

5. Guaranteed. One of the fears most human beings have is taking a risk. They want to know that if your product doesn't work out, they can get their money back.

6. Health. Remember the expression. "If I've got my health, I've got everything"? If a product promotes financial, emotional, or physical health, it offers a big plus. To many people, this feeling is even more important than money.

7. Love. Many companies make enormous amounts of money selling love.[11] Whether it's dating services or vacations for single people; love is always a prime selling hook.

8. New. If it's new, it must be better. It's a tried-and-true concept that seems to be part of the American mystique. And although there is always the occasional fiasco, like the New Coke debacle of a few years' back, we still like to think of ourselves as being on the cutting edge.

9. Proven. Although we like new things, we want reliability as well. We want something that has been tested and proven not to be harmful in any way. We also don't want something that will break down or require a lot of servicing. We don't want to doubt that something will work.

10. Results. Another twist to the Americans psyche. Although we may mouth the words, underneath we don't care about trying hard and putting forth our best efforts if we do not see results. We want to know exactly what we're getting for spending our money.

11. Safe. This closely parallels health. We all value our lives, and if a [11] product is safe, or our assets are safe. We are much more trusting.

12. Save. Saving money is almost as important as making money. If a company can't promise that you will make money with a product, it usually promises to assist you save money. Saving is better than spending.

13. Own. We all like to own things. Owning is better than buying, because it implies possession rather than more spending. When you present a product, talk about owning it rather than buying it.

14. Free. "Free" is an instant eye catcher, something that compels you to look further. If you can use free in any selling that you do, pointing out that your Prospect will get something for nothing, use it. You'll immediately get your Prospect's attention.

15. Best. If you know that a product has been shown to be the best in any way, shape, or form, be sure your Prospect is made aware of it. Possessing something that has been shown to be the best in mileage, has the best service record, has won a taste test exerts a very powerful pull to have it for ourselves.

16. Value. When you begin to talk about value the person inherently starts to construct images of times they have receive value with a product or service. So value is a very powerful word if used correctly. Since the word is over used by a lot of sales people make sure you use it with a "serious sincerity".

17. Improved. People always want something better than what they already have. The latest and greatest is assumed to be better than what is existing.

18. Unique. Everybody likes to feel special and different in some way. By just showing the prospect how the Prospect can reach a new improved level of uniqueness the Prospect will be intrigued. Usually, people do not like to be part of the pack.

Chapter 15 - Structure of Linguistic Presuppositions

15.1 Time and Future Pacing Presuppositions

Past	Present	Future
Back Then or Then	Now	When
Before	Here	After
Look Back	Already or Looking	Look Ahead
Just	During or While	Soon
Happened	Happen or Happening	Will Happen
Was	Is	Will be
Made	Will make	Will make
Did	Doing or Until	May or Want to
Decision	Decide or Deciding	Decided

The most popular time presuppositions are:

Before	**During**	**After**
When	**While**	**Soon**
As	**And**	**Now**

Time presuppositions are the words that drive the power of all future pace patterns. **Future pacing** is the process of mentally imagining oneself in a future situation with a newly acquired behavior, product and/or service. For example: One year from now, won't it be great after learning this information. Now thinking of all the amazing results.

Examples:

1. **As** you read this sentence you will start to think of all the people you know who need to take this course.

2. **After,** you finish the fourth example you will easily understand how to use all of the time presuppositions.

3. **Before,** you realize it you'll be talking to everyone about the unlimited power of this course.

4. **During and While** you're reading this sentence you will discover amazing new ways to use this information.

Process Information:

Prospect: Well, you're too late, we decided on another product.

You:

I realize that you did decide, but I am very, very curious; Now, how did you decide on that product.

What this technique does, is it takes a cemented decision and loosens it up, while simultaneously eliciting process information.

Future Pacing or Time Line Selling:

You: As you begin to think about all the applications this product will have in your life, now won't it be great after you have purchased this product and you are using it, and you have gained an even more profound appreciation for it, and just imagine ten years from now as you look back at today now and realize that by purchasing this product you have made the best decision possible.

The pattern first causes confusion by switching from the future to the present quickly. Secondly, during the delivery you are presupposing that the Prospect has already bought your product and they are feeling good about that decision.

You: Won't it be great, one year from now, looking back at today and realizing that this was the start of something special? And you can say to yourself, "HHMM – Going with this product was the best decision I have ever made." And after you have already accepted the fact that using this product can make you feel good, because you can now see the future as being much brighter it is pretty natural to accept this because you have this product in your life.

This pattern takes the person into the future and then simply makes them look back after they have already purchased your product and are satisfied using it. It fries their sense of time orientation.

15.2 - Cause and Effect Presuppositions

The structure of this category is easy to understand. In fact, by just reading this sentence, it will allow you to quickly understand how cause and effect presuppositions work. Before we get into the examples, remember all you have to do is link a truism "cause" to a presupposed "effect" that will get you closer, inside your clients' head, to the outcome you desire.

This structure is also the basis for structuring what Hypnotists call binds. Where a bind may be found in the second sentence in the first paragraph on this page.

So the structure is **"Some X will cause some Y result"**

By the way, there is no correlation between reading the second sentence in the first paragraph on this page and the speed at which you will gain a profound understanding of cause and effect presuppositions.

AS you are reading this sentence and thinking about

all the applications, **then you** can easily grasp the

concept of Cause and Effect Presuppositions

So in fact you have just learned four techniques within one example. The four techniques are:

1. **Truisms** which are also known as Rhetorical Statements (see page 18) in the above example, it would be "reading this sentence"

2. **Pacing** can be considered Stating a Truism or expressing Rhetorical Statements. Yet pacing has another unique application, which you will learn in the section discussing Verbal Pacing and Leading. In the above example, the first pace would be **"AS you** are reading this sentence." The second pace would be "and thinking". With a lead presupposition, you are specifically directing your client to access thoughts with regard to "all the applications."

3. The **Lead** in this example is also the **Effect.** In the above example **"you** can easily grasp the concept of Cause and Effect Presuppositions."

AS you are reading this sentence and thinking about

all the applications, **then you** can easily grasp the

concept of Cause and Effect Presuppositions.

---

4. For this example, the **Cause and Effect** structure begins with "**AS you**". The cause portion of the sentence is:

AS you are reading this sentence .....

And the word **"AS"** is being used as a temporal linkage word.

The best temporal linkage words used within cause and effect presupposition structures are: While, And, When, During & As. The effect portion of the sentence is:

..... then you can easily grasp the concept

of Cause and Effect Presuppositions

The presuppositions are:

thinking about all the applications

understanding the concept of Cause and Effect Presuppositions

---

Temporal Linkage words:

WHILE, AND, WHEN, DURING, BEFORE & AS

Causality words:

Causes	Forces	Requires	Makes
Because	Allows	Since	Determines
Proves	Creates	Reason	Justify

Cause and Effect Structures:

(Cause) makes (Effect)

If (Cause) then (Effect)

As you (Cause) then you (Effect)

Some X will cause you to feel some Y

During this class you will <u>notice</u> new things about language and by just noticing one thing, will <u>make</u> you want to look for even more applications.

If you are reading this sentence, *then* you are learning beyond your conscious awareness, **and** because everyone has an unconscious, it will naturally force you to understand it at a more deeper and profound level, **And** <u>since</u> this has already happened you can feel good.

This product will <u>allow</u> you to save an incredible amount of money, **and** after you have decided to buy it, you can naturally <u>allow</u> yourself to relax, because **while** you're using this product you will feel certain that you <u>made</u> the best decision by going with this product.

<u>Since</u> you are meeting with me, you will naturally glean a deeper understanding just how this product will completely transform your corporate image, <u>because</u> **as** you look ahead to the future **and** begin to imagine having a work-force that has all above average players, then your job will become pleasurable.

Thinking about these patterns will <u>cause</u> you to get excited **and** this means you are quickly learning **and** letting your imagination run wild **as** you discover the unlimited power of this information.

15.3 - AWARENESS PRESUPPOSITIONS

AWARENESS WORDS ARE VERY, VERY POWERFUL, PROVIDING THAT EVERYTHING THAT FOLLOWS THE AWARENESS WORD IS PRESUPPOSED TOWARD YOUR OUTCOME.

Realize	Aware	Understand
Know	Notice	Experience
Think	Feel	Wonder
Discover	Grasp	Consider
Assume	Weigh	Perceive

When constructing your sentence you have the flexibility to add "ing" to the end of these words.

Examples

I personally, get excited, when I **perceive** value. With me, the value that a product gives you, should outweigh the investment, and simultaneously give you that **feeling** of satisfaction. It's like you can automatically **realize** that you have made a good decision by buying this product.

The slightest **awareness** of just how good this information is, will lead you to a feeling complete excitement.

I can't say that you will **realize** that this is the best product for you, yet I have been told by some Prospects that by just **considering** the ownership of it, they develop a feel of ease. Easily realizing that the decision was over as to whether they are going to buy this product or not. Then they were able to look forward to using this product and have that feel of satisfaction.

As you begin to construct, inside your mind, all the wonderful benefits that you will **experience** by simply owning this product, you can **notice** how much better you are already feeling, Now let's .....

Because you are **realizing** the amazing value of owning this product

Are you starting to **experience** the satisfaction of what owning this will bring you?

15.4 - Adjective / Adverb Presuppositions

When using Adjectives and Adverbs, use your voice by pronouncing the Adjective and Adverbs with a soft smooth texture combined with higher pitched tone.

When pronouncing the nouns and verbs lower your voice and slow down your voice tempo. It also assists when you see a sentence fragment.

Examples:

We have *Soft, Comfortable* **Shirts.**

This car will give you a *Smooth, Safe* **Ride.**

A person can *Quickly and Easily* **Become Excited.**

This *Accurate, Comprehensive* **Report ...**

This *entertaining and fascinating* **Course,** will ...

Always place the ADJECTIVES and ADVERBS before the NOUNS and VERBS.

Quickly	Automatically	Amazing	Profound
Rich	Immediately	Naturally	Already
Unlimited	Easily	Continue	Happily
Fortunately	Luckily	Obviously	Stop
Infinity	Repeatedly	Usually	Yet
Truly	Still	Start	Continue
Begin	Any More	Some	Most
Finally	All		

Example:

Obviously, everything is **beginning** to become clear, and **naturally** you can **quickly** realize how this will change your life for the better.

Example:

Truly, this is the best course in the world. I believe this to be true. Don't you?

Finally, you may **continually** think about how **easily** you can refer people to this amazing course.

15.5 Spatial Presuppositions

Spatial presuppositions cause powerful relationships between things such as products, choices, services, options thoughts and ideas.   Spatial presuppositions also give the illusion of choice.

Across	After	Among
Between	Down	Away
Inside	Onto	Touching
By	Under	Round
Beyond	Above	Through
Without	Toward	Further
Beneath	Including	Within
Out of	Below	From Below
Without	Close(er)	In front of
Expanded	In	In Place of
Without	Along with	Relative to
Against	From Under	From Behind
At	Along	From Above

Off	Beside	Aside From
Outside	On	Apart From
Over	That	Near(er)
Here	Around	Off the top
Into	Uncover	

Examples:

Placing that issue <u>aside</u> now for a moment, is there anything in addition to that?

<u>Between</u> quality, saving time, or saving money, which would be the most important benefit to you?

<u>Among</u> all the positive warm feelings that you are already having, I am certain that there is one reason <u>above</u> all the rest; which one is causing you to realize that this should be implemented immediately?

Chapter 16 - Embedded Commands

Commands

* Now   * Start

* Stop   * Begin

Verbal Pacing and Leading

Pacing and Leading is one of the most powerful yet discreet and subtle persuasion techniques that exist. You have been exposed to Physiology Pacing and Leading in the Calibration Section and Pacing and Leading in the Cause and Effect Presupposition Section. Now, you are going to be exposed to the Verbal Pacing and Leading Technique. When you utilize the verbal pacing and leading technique you just pace your client with truisms or undisputable facts about reality and after the client is in a deep rapport with you, you then methodically blend in leading presupposition that will allow you to achieve your outcome.

Pacing and Leading Structure:

Pace (1), Pace (2) Pace (3) Pace (4):

Pace (1), Pace (2) Pace (3) Lead (1):

Pace (1), Pace (2) Lead (1) Lead (2):

Pace (1), Lead (1) Lead (2) Lead (3):

Lead (1), Lead (2) Lead (3) Lead (4):

Let's read this example of Pacing and Leading:

Obviously you are looking at this page and you know this course is called Quantum Selling. You have just learned about commands and now you are learning about verbal pacing and leading. So as you are learning about verbal pacing and leading, I am sure it is apparent to you that you are reading from left to right, and allowing your eyes to take in the information, so you can start to think positively about this information. Within this positive realization, as you are reading and following each word, you can relax, because you've become aware of all the amazing concepts. In fact, by only understanding one concept from this course, one can automatically get excited and feel

about all the incredible possibilities. Now, any new possibility can quickly allow you to have new insights. And even one powerful insight could affect your future in a tremendous way.

Pace (1), Pace (2) Pace (3) Pace (4):

Looking at this page (1),

called Quantum Selling (2),

learned about commands (3),

learning about verbal pacing and leading (4)

Pace (1), Pace (2), Pace (3), Lead (1):

as you are learning about pacing and leading (1)

Reading from left to right (2),

eyes take in the information (3),

think positively (1)

Pace (1), Pace (2), Lead (1), Lead (2):

within this positive realization (1),

reading and following each word (2),

can relax (1),

aware of amazing concepts (2)

Pace (1), Lead (1), Lead (2), Lead (3):

Understanding one concept from this course (1),

automatically get excited (1),

feel enthusiastic (2),

incredible possibilities (3)

Lead (1), Lead (2), Lead (3), Lead (4):

any new possibility (1),

have new insights (2),

one powerful insight (3),

affect your future in a tremendous way (4)

Notice the subtle structure of this technique; the ending of one-section runs into the beginning of the next section. By overlapping you achieve two powerful effects: *first,* it strengthens the pacing pattern so it is difficult for the unconscious to distinguish between where one pace begins and the pace or lead starts; *secondly,* it further pounds in the beginning paces or the beginning lead. This structure naturally causes unconscious agreement. The technique will quickly get you to your outcome.

16.1 - *Structure of Embedded Commands* That Direct States and Emotions

The Purpose of Embedded Commands are to direct your client into the state that will allow them to behave in a manner that will allow your client to achieve his/her outcome and you to achieve your outcome. To directly give a command, to most people, would elicit resistance. Embedded commands allow you to talk to a person's unconscious without conscious awareness. The structure of an embedded command is as follows:

Structure of an Embedded Command that Directs States:

CBP + CV + SPE

Embedded Command means putting a command inside of a sentence.

C.B.P. Conscious By-Pass Phrase is to set-up your command and shut down the conscious mind's filters so the command can slide straight through to the unconscious.

C.V. Command Verb is the function that you want the unconscious mind to perform.

S.P.E. State, Process or Experience is the feelings you want to elicit, (bring to the conscious). The state should be congruent with the outcome you want.

C.B.P.

When you ...
If I were to ...
A Person Can ...
It's not necessary to ...
You don't have to ...
What would it be (feel) like if ...
To the point where ...
Notice what it's like ...
If you were to ...
What's it like when (to) ...
As you ...
You really shouldn't ...
I Invite you to notice ...
Have you ever ...
You can find (yourself) ...
Can you ...
How do you ...
When were you best able ...
When was the last time ...
What happens as you ...
I hope you will ...

C.V.

Become
Get
Have
Experience
Forget
Know
Think About
Remember
Fall
Consider

S.P.E.

Confidence	Desire
Comfort	Security
Curiosity	Joy
Confusion	Delight
Certainty	Need
Good	Happy
Excited	Delighted

Priority Command Verbs

Priority Command Verbs are the best verbs that automatically and naturally cause trans-derivational searches.

Instantaneously
Immediately
Find Yourself
Suddenly
Picture
Suppose
Convince Yourself
Realize
Ponder
Mysterious
Imagine
Remember
Wonder
Allow Yourself

Note: Your voice should match the feeling the SPE describes

	C.B.P.	C.V.	S.P.E.
1	_____	_____	_____
2	_____	_____	_____
1	_____	_____	_____
1	_____	_____	_____

Why is it important to direct your client into a state before directing them to take action?

Because all sales are first decided upon by UNCONSCIOUS EMOTION, and afterward justified by conscious logic. People find what emotionally pleases them first; then they rationalize their feelings. In family counseling, most family conflicts are first created by one person having his/her feelings hurt. Then that person, who first had his/her feelings hurt, responds with some consequential action. You now understand this consequential action as an emotional response.

Have you ever heard any of the following statements from a significant other:

"If you would do X, then I wouldn't do Z."

Translation: When you do X; then I feel Y, and then I do the action of Z.

"When you do X, then I feel Y."

"If you would just do X then I wouldn't xo Z (action)."

Remember:

Every Decision is Driven by

Emotions and justified by Logic and

Rational after the decision is made.

Now, here is how most salespeople get confused with this aforementioned notion: A Prospect says, "I need to make a logical decision in order to find out if your product makes a sense for me." At this point some salespeople assume or hallucinate that the client is going to perhaps weigh out all the features, benefits, prices, options, and consequences of your product.

WRONG!!   This Prospect is simply looking for a **feeling of intelligence**, which would **"make sense"** to them.

So never, never confuse a logical decision process for a feeling of intelligence.

16.2 - Structure of Embedded Commands That will Direct Action

The formal technical structure of an embedded command

First   Decide exactly what it is you want them to do.

             Select a pre-determine outcome.

Second   Develop Sentence(s).   But before developing your
             sentence, understand that the formal   technical
             structure of an embedded command is usually a two
             word means, immediately followed by one or more end.
             **You must stack or deliver at least three pre-
             suppositions in a single sentence or verbal
             expression.** This structure will cause the result.

Third   Deliver the embedded command.

Fourth   Using Sensory Acuity, Calibrate for Outcome or Results

Two Word Means	One Word End
How to Do It	What to Do
+ (action or state)	

You *can* **feel**	Happy
I hope you *will* **get**	Excited
A person *can* **become**	Relaxed
If you were *to* **fall into**	Agreement
Would you **consider**	Buying
I hope you **feel**	Certain

The two most common ways to build

"Action" Embedded Commands:

First   The infinitive "to" followed by an embedded command. Where the embedded command is not greater than three to four words.

Second   Any "modal operator" followed by an embedded command. Where the embedded command is not greater than three to four words.

MODAL OPERATORS LIST

Negative Necessity	*Necessity*
Doesn't Allow	Allow
Don't have to	Got to
Got to not	Have to
It's not time	It's time
Must not	Must
Not Necessary	Necessary
Ought not	Ought to
Shouldn't	Should
Supposed not to	Supposed to

IMPROBABILITY

Couldn't	Don't dare to	Don't Deserve
Don't let	Don't prefer	Don't pretend
Don't wish	Had better not	May Not
Might not		

PROBABILITY

Could	Dare to	Deserve
Had better	Let	May
Might	Prefer	Pretend
Wish	Would	

POSSIBILITY

Able to	Am	Can
Choose to	Decide	Do
Intend	It is possible	Permit
Try	Will	

IMPOSSIBILITY

Am not	Can't	Doesn't permit
Don't Choose to	Don't Decide	Don't intend
Impossible	Try not	Unable to
Won't		

States, Processes & Experiences in selling and persuading:

Confidence	Comfort (ability)	Ease – Easy
Certain (y)	Excite (ment/ing)	Desire (ing)
Love	Connection	Compulsion
Fascination	Obsession	Like (ness)
Enjoy (ment)	Pleasure (able)	Sumptuous
Trust	Respect	Piece of Mind
Secure (ity)	Intelligence	Satisfaction
Commitment	Loyalty	Pride
Excellence	Good	Happy
Delight	Smart	Safe
Fairness	Eager	Win (ner/ning)
Intrigue	Curious	Enthusiastic
Chemistry		

16.3 – Focus

When communicating with anyone always have a clear, concise outcome in mind. Without a precise focused outcome you are engaging in small talk. In other words focus your thoughts and language toward what you do want and forget about what you don't want.

Before you engage someone to persuade ask yourself:

"What outcome do I specifically want from the interaction?"
"What must I first feel in order to lead them into a state that will allow them to do what I want?"

"What emotional state must I elicit in them first, which will allow my client to enter the state which will allow me to achieve my outcome?"

16.4 - Softeners

A softener(s) is a preeminent introduction; also know as light fluff talk which softens the client's conscious mind so you can easily enter into a conversation concerning your outcome.

Just for conversation sake

I am curious as to

I am just wondering whether

I ask myself

Softener – Embedded Commands

- **Sometime........**

Emotion: Sometime, people *like us* just want to *feel connected* to someone who naturally understands needs like ours.....

Action: Sometime, people who *quickly buy* this product, feel certain that it's the best product on the market even before they talk with me face to face.

- **Eventually.......**

Emotion: Eventually, people allow themselves the comfort of giving into all those wonderful feelings of certainty, Certainty in realizing that.....

Action: Eventually, sometimes during our conversation, **here you will** experience a sudden awareness about the amazing benefits of this product, which will cause you to perhaps feel compelled to go with this product.

- **Sooner or later........**

Emotion: Sooner or later, you will come to realize how much piece of mind one can have owning this product now will give you....

Action: Sooner or later, by fulfilling your desire for owning his product you can only then, (physically sigh) sigh that sigh of satisfaction

- **I'm wondering if........**

Emotion: I'm wondering if you have ever feel comfortable with someone you have met for the first time now?.....

Action: I'm wondering if you are ready to buy this product

Statement – Embedded Commands

- **A person could [*Client Name*], _____.**

Emotion: A person could, John, *feel comfortable*

Action: A person could, John, *buy this product* and

- **A person might [*Client Name*], _____.**

Emotion: A person might, *John, feel compelled* to.....

Action: A person might, *John, purchase* this for

- **A person _____, because .....**

Emotion: A person can *desire this course......*

Action: A person will *feel compelled* to refer their friends to me, because of the power of the information.

- **One may, [*Client Name*], _____,**

Emotion: One may, *John, forget* about past negative experiences....

Action: One may, *John, sign* this contract.....

- **A person is able to** _____.

Emotion: A person is able to *become absolutely satisfied......*

Action: A person is able to quickly *decide on this product*

- **People can, you know,** _____.

Emotion: People can, you know easily *have confidence, **by*** buying this product because of all the benefits.....

Action: People can, you know make a commitment to refer your friends to me.....

Emotion: People can, you know, experience total pleasure with this product because.....

Action: People can, you know, quickly buy this product due to the incredible feelings of delight.....

Statement – Embedded Commands

- **One can** _____, **because......**

Emotion: One can, naturally *become fascinated,* because......

Action: One can, readily and easily *acquire this product,* because...

- **When you** _____, **then.....**

Emotion: When you imagine yourself using this product, then you can ultimately experience true delight.....

Action: When you buy this product, then you will be making a statement, a statement that says sign me up for the future

- **Maybe you'll** _____.

Emotion: Maybe you'll become obsessed with owning this product...

Action: Maybe you'll agree with everything I am telling you, or maybe you won't

- **I invite you to notice the feelings ... as you ...**

Emotion and Action: I invite you to notice that you can have that feeling of security, as you consider buying this product now .....

- **I invite you to notice the sensation in ... while you ...**

Emotion and Action: I invite you to notice the sensation of delight while you begin to experience owning this product.....

- **You can _____, because ...**

Emotion: You can have that feeling of intelligence because...

Action: You can feel good as you buy this product because it comes with a one-year money back guarantee.....

Emotion & Action: You can have that feeling of intelligence because of the research we have done on this product yet that's not the best part, the best part is the incredible feeling you're going to have, sooner than you think. You see this product can .....

- **You probably already have realized.....**

Emotion: You probably already have realized that our Prospects feel satisfied.....

Action: You probably already have realized how easy it is to have this product and after you own this product.....

- **You are able to _____.**

Emotion: You are able to enjoy yourself even more after you own this product.....

Action: You are able to imagine owning this product cause of the strong need.....

- **You may _____.**

Emotion: You may allow yourself to come to trust me because of the great referrals that I am going to how you now.....

Action: You may get excited before you buy this product.....

- **One can, [*Client Name*], _____.**

Emotion: One can, *John be at ease......*

Action: One can, *John, immediately buy......*

Questions – Embedded Commands

- **What happens when you _____?**

Emotion: What happens when you're excited about a product?

Action: What happens when you are absolutely convinced that this is the best product for you?

- **Will you _____ now, or will you _____?**

Emotion: Will you fall in love with this product now just by looking at it, or will you fall in love with it after you buy it?

Action: Will you buy now, or will you decide to buy in a moment or two?

- **Will you ..., or ..., or ..., ?**

Emotion: Will you become fascinated by using this product or just obsessed with it owning one of these?

Action: Will you buy from me today or do you need to think about it for a minute and then buy from me?

- **What happens when you _____ ?**

Emotion: What happens when you're exhilarated with the notion of owning this product?

Action: What happens when you decide this is the best product for you?

- **How interested are you in _____ ?**

    Emotion: How interested are you in feeling happy?

Action: How interested are you in owning this product to save money or are you more interested in saving time or perhaps quality?

- **Imagine _____ ?**

Emotion: Imagine how happy you are feeling after you have this product?

Action: Imagine owning this product and being the envy of everyone else?

- **Do you really think you can enjoy _____ ?**

Emotion & Action: Do you really think you can enjoy owning a product like this, especially years and years to come?

Questions with Negation – Embedded Commands

- **You can _____, can you not?**

Emotion: You can have that feeling of intelligence when you own product, can you not?

Action: You can easily by now, see yourself with this product, can you not?

- **It's easy to _____, is it not?**

Emotion & Action: It's easy to have fun and convince yourself that this is the best product for you, is it not?

Negation – Embedded Commands

- **One doesn't have to, [*Client Name*], _____.**

Emotion: One doesn't have to, John, desire this product. Only need it.

Action: One doesn't have to buy immediately.

- **A person may not realize _____.**

Emotion: A person may not realize those rich feelings of happiness with this product.

Action: A person may not realize how quickly they can decide.

- **People don't have to, [*Client Name*], _____.**

Emotion: People don't have to, John, feel pleasure with this product, just blind overwhelming lust for this product

Action: People don't have to, John, buy now, you can wait a minute or two

- **One doesn't have to, [*Client Name*], _____.**

Emotion: One doesn't have to, John, settle on this product

Action: One doesn't have to, John, settle on this product

- **Don't _____.**

Emotion: Don't believe everything I say, check it out for yourself, I'm not God.

Action: Don't forget about my competition

Negation – Embedded Commands

- **Maybe you haven't ...... yet.**

Emotion: Maybe you haven't have that feeling of delight ... yet

Action: Maybe you haven't discovered this is the best for you ... yet

- **You may not realize _____.**

Emotion: You may not realize that feel of delightful pleasure by owning this product. You see ...

Action: You may not realize all the value within this product. So let me ask you ...

- **You don't have to _____.**

Emotion: You don't have to believe everything I am saying, yet we only have to agree on ...

Action: You don't have to buy now.

- **You may or may not _____.**

Emotion: You may or may not understand the incredible feeling of pride you can have owning this product.

Action: You may or may not decide on the $10,000 retainer.

- **I don't know if _____.**

Emotion: I don't know if you have that comfortable sensation that will make you feel certain

Action: I don't know if you have convinced yourself that this is the best product, so …

Negation – Embedded Commands

- **I wouldn't tell you to _____, because …**

Emotion: I wouldn't tell you to think about all the pleasure you can have by owning this product, because if you knew what other Prospects have said you couldn't hold yourself back from buying this product for even a second.

Action: I wouldn't tell you to consider buying this product, because all of your questions may not be completely satisfied. Now, what were you saying?

- **I'm wondering if you'll _____ … or not.**

Emotion: I'm wondering if you'll feel excellent about this product more before you purchase it or not.

Action: I'm wondering if you'll have all your expectations exceeded with this product or not.

Quotes – Embedded Commands

This is an interesting pattern; it's used to deliver a message that is embedded in quotations, as if someone else had stated the message.

This pattern gives complete and total flexibility because you can literally say anything you want to say and claim that someone else said it.

- ... said, "_____."

Example: XYZ company, said "If people don't buy immediately from you they should have their heads examined." I like to think they are right yet it is a strong statement.

Quotes – Embedded Commands

- ... one told me, "_____."

Example: A client once told me "WOW, referring to this product, I need to buy now, because if it produces half the results you say it can it has got to be good."

The best way to define what a Linguistical Ambiguity is, is to simply give you an example of the two most powerful types of ambiguities for sales: Phonological and Punctuation.

Chapter 17 – Ambiguities

17.1 Phonological Ambiguities

- Buy for now = Buy Four Now

- Bye now = By now = Buy Now, you can ...

- By and By = Buy and Buy

- your mind = you're mine

17.2 Punctuation Ambiguities

- You **WANT Me** to explain ...

- **Like me,** I agree ...

- **As you, Like, ...**

- As you think about **pride. To me,** I think ...

- ... and **feel comfortable? Now, with me ...**

- ... ever **like somebody? Me ...**

Tag Questions:

- Is this what you would like to do?

- Are you with me?

Linguistic Twists:

- Celebration and Sale = "Salibration"

Chapter 18 – Summary

The Sales / Persuasion Cycle REVIEW

- ☉ **Capture Attention – Get Interest and 100% of Prospects Attention**

- ☉ **Induction of Collaborative Cooperation Between You and the Client**

- ☉ **Collect and Gather Client Buying Criteria and Strategy**

- ☉ **Combine and Package Client Information Interweaving in your Product and / or Service**

- ☉ **Turn Client into Sales Representative for You**

- ☉ **Sign Contract / Take Money / Get Purchase Order**

Capture Attention – Get Interest and Attention

-- State to be induced: curiosity, intrigue, surprise, fascination

» Techniques in Prospecting: Mailings, Cold Calling, Canvassing, Signs, Gifts, Flowers, Notes, Video with you in the video explaining the product and/or service, A Cake, A Sales Letter

» Techniques in Front of **Prospect:** Pattern Interrupts, Money

• Explain what you can do for the client within 60 seconds

√ **Outcome: On the Phone Sell the Appointment and Set appointment,**

√ **Outcome: In front of the Prospect, Rivet 100% of his/her attention on you.**

On the phone:

John, this is Joe, I'm with SF Inc. John, currently my company is working with such companies as " Buyer ", " Zip " and " Mac ", and we have assisted these companies reduce turnover, increase productivity which ultimately has allowed them to enjoy greater profits.

We have assisted these companies achieve these goals with a psychometric instrument which has a myriad of applications such as:

We have assisted " Zip ", match their sales reps which has led to an 8% increase in sale performance...

We have assisted " Mac ", with their admin which has led to $100,000 dollar savings annually.

John, I don't know if you will met with me, yet I would like to see if you can naturally squeeze me into your calendar for a quick 15 minute appointment.

In front of the Prospect:

Before we get into this process of whether (Heavy Deep Sign) you're going to buy this product or not, which will allow you to make a decision as to whether this is the best product for you or whether this is something you're going to use, and at this point I'm not sure if you will believe everything I tell you, yet, it makes me feel better by saying that I hope you can feel my genuine sincerity and professionalism as we go through this process to allow you to discover for yourself as to whether this is a good product for you, or not so as I explain to you; if you need clarification on any point just stop me. Are you with me?

State to be induced: confidence, trust, likeness, respect, comfort, certainty

» Techniques: Rapport, Verbal and Physiology Pacing, Mirroring and Matching, Language Patterns

» PRESUPPOSITION FOCUSED AT OUTCOME (MIXING IN NEGATION)

• What to look for in order to understand the process: Head nodding, they repeat your language, they begin to relax and you are able to visually notice it, facial color healthy pink, and skin tone with pores becoming larger

RELAXED ZONED OUT STATE BEGINNING

√ **Outcome: When calibrating your client follows your leads, they tell you that they feel good or positive about being with you**

Negotiation Model:

First Step: Is to chunk up until you achieve agreement on a specific issue. You have achieved the outcome of agreement when you and the other person have used the same word.

(Chunking is the organizing or breaking down some experience into bigger or smaller pieces. Chunking up involves moving to a larger, more abstract level of information. Chunking down involves moving to a more specific and concrete level of information.   Chunking literally involves finding other examples at another level of information.)

Second Step: Is to separate intention from behavior.

- Use a conditional close – test

- So if you get X then however we – operate

- Do it – test exit

Third Step: Is to chunk down only as quickly as you can maintain agreement.

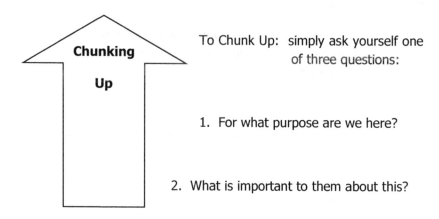

To Chunk Up: simply ask yourself one
of three questions:

1. For what purpose are we here?

2. What is important to them about this?

3. How can I exaggerate this?

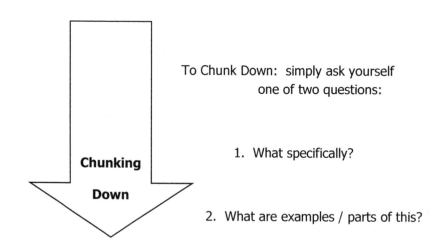

To Chunk Down: simply ask yourself
one of two questions:

1. What specifically?

2. What are examples / parts of this?

After Thoughts?

The President Selling the Country on HIS Agenda

The presidential election in the United States of America is, I believe, the single biggest sales pitch in the world. Hypnotic language was the one enormous tool that the current president used to secure both election and re-elections. When you analyze the transcripts of his speeches this becomes very apparent.

Hypnotic can be defined as something so fascinating that the attention of people watching or listening is absorbed completely. Other terms used by the media explicitly and implicitly say the same thing. The speech was Mesmerizing, spellbinding, soothing, fascinating, magnetic. They were also *__repetitive and rhythmic__* which is by definition hypnotic. They were repetitive not only in the sense of theme but also in the use of certain vague (Hypnotic Words). Even the slogans were explicitly chosen for this purpose. HOPE AND CHANGE are two words that the candidate NEVER defined and will never. If they were made explicit then they would lose their power. By keeping Hope And Change vague, everyone could put in their OWN meaning. Even when the words "YOU CAN BELIEVE IN" were added, the phrase Hope and Change You Can Believe In means nothing. The second campaign slogan was chosen for the same emotional and hypnotic reason. FORWARD. Now this word implies many thing things depending on content. Remember the English language is very content dependent. Forward was not defined and it implies anything else, i.e., the other party must be Backwards. In his book "Dream FROM My Father" he made it clear what his agenda and beliefs are.

Another favorite hypnotic tool of the speech writers, whoever they are, is the phrase "it's just like" and the variations thereof. If I had a son he would look just like Travon Martin.....

A look at his first speech in Cairo contained 37 "BUTS" in just four pages. You may remember "BUTS". Johnny, you are a good worker BUT. Jane, you are a sweet girl, BUT. Thirty seven times "America is GOOD, BUT" and "Islam is BAD, BUT" was contained in that speech. The pattern has not changed in five years. Let me be perfectly clear, do you have any hope that it will change to one you can believe in and move forward?

References

1 – James, Tad. NLP Master Practitioner Training. Advanced Neuro Dynamics, Inc. & Tad James, 1988, 1989, p. 3

2 – Dilts, Robert. Changing Beliefs Systems with NLP. Cupertino, California: Meta Publications, 1990, p. 1

3 – Bagley, Dan and Reese, Edward. Beyond Selling. Cupertino, California: Meta Publications, 1988, pp. 14-28

4 – Bagley, Dan and Reese, Edward. Beyond Selling. Cupertino, California: Meta Publications, 1988, pp. 6-14

5 – Bagley, Dan and Reese, Edward. Beyond Selling. Cupertino, California: Meta Publications, 1988, p. 43

6 – Johnson, Kerry. Sales Magic. New York, New York: Nightingale-Conant Corporation, 1994, p. 32

7 – Johnson, Kerry. Sales Magic. New York, New York: Nightingale-Conant Corporation, 1994, p. 37

8 – Johnson, Kerry. Sales Magic. New York, New York: Nightingale-Conant Corporation, 1994, p. 43

9 – Bagley, Dan and Reese, Edward. Beyond Selling. Cupertino, California: Meta Publications, 1988, p. 56

10 – Bagley, Dan and Reese, Edward. Beyond Selling. Cupertino, California: Meta Publications, 1988, pp. 63-66

11 – Bagley, Dan and Reese, Edward. Beyond Selling. Cupertino, California: Meta Publications, 1988, pp. 67-77

12 – Johnson, Kerry. Sales Magic. New York, New York: Nightingale-Conant Corporation, 1994, p. 43

Quantum Selling Flash Cards

You, like me, were probably raised to believe that selling was logical. Just present the facts, the features, the specs, the benefits in a logical, sensible way and the potential customer will buy. Have you ever been in a sales situation where the salesperson was perfect, the sales pitch was perfect, every objection was answered, every question was answered and the customer still did NOT BUY? Have you ever wondered why? What goes through your mind when one customer buys and what seemed like the same exact situation with another and they did not buy? Want the answer? Well, here it is in simple English again.

ALL SALES ARE EMOTIONAL SALES

That's right buster or madam, which ever you happen to be, if you cannot or do not reach the potential customer on the emotional level your doomed.

QUANTUM SELLING IS AN ANSWER

Now, before you consider attending our live course, I want to explain a couple of things. Most salespeople have one or more of the following limiting beliefs.

The general consensus in this nation is that salespeople are bad. You were raised with the used car salesman shark as the role model, and no one wants to be thought of in those terms. A large portion of the sales force out there today are there, not because they want to be, serving the customer, it because they have to be for whatever reason. Have you ever met a salesperson you liked? Now as you think about that person and the qualities they have, do you think you could be that type of sales person? If so, then you're on your way to success with the information in this book.

Interestingly enough most people including sales people also have a belief in their head about how much they are worth. What do I mean by this? Of course, I mean they think of themselves as worth $50,000 or $100,000 and that's what they earn. A $50,000 dollar (self-worth) sales person has been given new more lucrative territory and now earns $50,000 in half the time NOT $100,000 in the same time. If you have a limiting belief about your own self-worth, forget this course. You are stuck and we certainly don't want you to earn just the same amount in half the time NOW DO WE.

And then there is the famous belief in product. It has been said that if you do not use the product you can't sell it. HOG WASH. Did you ever wonder what would happen if crane salespeople had to own and operate a crane before they could sell them. NOW there is a difference between owning and believing and you do have to believe in your product. If you believe your product is too expensive then YOU have the problem with money and not necessarily the person in front of you. If you feel your product is second best and everyone should only buy the best. You have the problem not the person to whom you are pitching.

NOW the reason that person who heard the perfect pitch didn't buy is because they could tell that the salesperson did not have their best interest at heart. If you are not willing to find out about that person on the emotional level and put the above beliefs aside then the Quantum Selling is not for you. STOP reading, will only cause yourself to live in delusion. Miracles can only be worked with those who believe in miracles. Watch the Steve Martin movie "Leap of Faith" and then notice how you feel about selling. This course is as much about you as it is them.

Super Influence Pattern #1

1. Entrain attention

2. Induce state

3. Amplify & intensify state

4. Link to action

Simple enough - get 'em fixated, start 'em going, get 'em to step on the gas and link to what you want 'em to do!

Super - Influence Pattern #2

1. Have you ever X?

2. Give Example

3. Describe process

4. Optional

amplifier: move sub-modalities This is most useful for complex processes that you want them to run when you aren't even around. Remember, the distinction between a tame animal and a trained animal. A trained animal will obey in its master's presence. A tame animal carries its master's voice around with it on the inside of its head and will obey even when the master isn't around

Super Conscious By-Pass Phrase #1

Have you ever

The THREE MOST POWERFUL words in the world! To ask a person, "have you ever" is actually commanding them to go inside and remember when they did, re-experiencing all those feelings! A powerful, no, super powerful way to induce states, triggers processes and influence at all levels! "Have you ever experienced incredible excitement, thinking about mastering new skills?"

Super Conscious By-Pass Phrase #2

What's it like when

This super weasel phrase serves the same function as super phrase #1 - Asking "What's it like" forces the person to go in and recall the circumstance, state or condition. "What's it like when you are absolutely certain that this product is right for you?

Quantum Seller Rule #1

Always communicate with an outcome in mind!

When you talk to a client don't do it just to be flapping your lips! Think of the states you want them in then use your skills to direct them!

Quantum Seller Rule #2

The purpose of your communication is to get you a sale!

The purpose of your communication is not to give the client an understanding. The purpose of your communication is to get you a sale! Quantum Selling works by manipulating and directing unconscious processes not by getting their conscious agreement. Leave convincing to your competition!

Quantum Seller Rule #3

Quantum Selling is fun!

The best magic is playfully done! If you aren't having fun with it, it isn't Quantum Selling!

Quantum Seller Rule #4

Keep your skills a secret!

Quantum Selling works because it is hidden and undetectable. True at very advanced levels you can tell them what you're doing and it will <u>still</u> work, but why give them the chance? Your aim is to <u>get a sale</u>, not impress with what you know.

Quantum Seller Rule #5

Be a stainless steel fist in a velvet glove!

Always be as low key as possible in application of your skills. Not "ha - ha I'm doing this thing to you" but "isn't it interesting how the mind works?" Soften, soften, and soften some more.

Quantum Seller Rule #6

Always go from least intrusive to most intrusive

Don't start right off moving their internal pictures! Do it, only after first exciting them with language patterns and/or anchoring. The best sales people spend 80 % of their time building rapport and 20 % closing.

Quantum Seller Rule #7

Don't resist what a client says ... turn it around and use it as leverage

Always use what is given - if they resist you by saying "I'm not ready" don't ask why! Find out "how" do you know? This will surprise them, disrupt and interrupt the objection so you can then lead them back to where you want them to be.

Quantum Seller Rule #8

Challenge is where the fun is!

What doesn't or isn't working is the doorway to new fun and power. Quantum Selling grew out of things not working forcing me to look for what did! Remember be tenacious as long as they need it, can afford it and it is the right thing for them.

Quantum Seller Rule #9

TONALITY IS EVERYTHING

Your tone of voice (inner and outer) must match your words! If you use a high, squeaky, irritating voice when you say "life's pleasures" you'll just blow it! Learn to control your voice tone!

Quantum Seller Rule #10

You can't get the client in their state unless you first get you in your state!

Quantum Selling depends on you first being rooted in a powerful, alive, upbeat, confident state! Work on your hypnosis tape, affirmations, visualization homework & breathing exercises to insure you'll be where you need to be to put the client where they needs to be.

Quantum Seller Rule #11

Train 'em and Tame 'em!

If it's only for the short term, then training them (getting them hot for your product or service when you want them to be) is enough. Long term you want them tamed - thinking of you in special ways even when you aren't there!

Quantum Seller Rule #12

Pride and Commitment

These are the two most important words in getting your customer to refer clients to you.

Quantum Seller Rule #13

Decisions or Not

Decisions are continually being mad and remade. People have bad days, good days and confusing days. One reject one day could lead to a million dollars another day and you have the ability to change their days.

Conscious By-Pass Phrase #1

When you ...

"When you" presupposes that you're going to do the thing discussed or enter the state so it's no longer open to debate. "When you get incredibly excited about a product do you find yourself compelled to buy it instantaneously or do you take a day to realize it is the best thing for you?"

Conscious By-Pass Phrase #2

What would it be like if ...

This statement is in effect a command for the person to imagine the condition or occurrence named or described after it. "What would it be like if you were to remember when you had products that allowed you to have that thrill of owning them?"

Conscious By-Pass Phrase #3

A person can

By talking about a "person's" experience it deflects any resistance on the part of your subject since you aren't really talking about them. "A person can become completely assured by only looking at the logic yet there is more!"

Conscious By-Pass Phrase #4

If you were to ...

This is a really useful Conscious By-Pass phrase! By saying "if", you deflect resistance while at the same time directing the person to imagine experiencing the condition, feeling or behavior. "If you were to not buy this immediately, how much money will it cost you?"

Conscious By-Pass Phrase #5

As you ...

This phrase presupposes the person will do the behavior or undergo the experience. "As you decide this is something you want to buy you will have a feeling of certainty."

Conscious By-Pass Phrase #6

It's not necessary to ...

An example of negation - by saying your command isn't necessary to - dissipates any resistance. "It's not necessary for you to look at this product through the eyes of positive feelings and focus upon having this product."

Conscious By-Pass Phrase #7

You really shouldn't

Another negation pattern you can use. Since you're saying they shouldn't, it's not like you're trying to get them to do it, aren't you! (In a playful tone of voice) "You really shouldn't think about buying this product, you don't want to be totally satisfied!"

Conscious By-Pass Phrase #8

You might find (yourself)

Useful as, the <u>start</u> of an intensifying chain of phrases, it implies that they're going to experience what you describe as something that just happens, so not only can they <u>not</u> resist it, but it implies that <u>you</u> had nothing to do with it! "You might find that a picture of you owning this product and having an unfair advantage over everyone ... "

Conscious By-Pass Phrase #9

to the point where ...

Really, this phrase connects one thing they are experiencing with the next thing you want them to experience - so it's useful both as a connector and amplifier. "You might find those pictures start to get bigger and brighter to the point where you forget about everything except owning this product."

Conscious By-Pass Phrase #10

Invite you to notice

Same effect as "you might find " - implies that what you describe is going to happen. Plus, "invite" has pleasant connotations of it being voluntary and polite!

"And I invite you to notice the wonderful feeling you are having NOW as you are thinking about putting these principles to work for you."

Conscious By-Pass Phrase #11

Notice what it's like

Same effect as "invite you to notice". It implies that the condition or experience is going to take place. This is very useful for moving people's internal pictures. "Notice what it's like as that picture of owning this product NOW, for whatever mysterious reason, pops itself into that location.

Conscious By-Pass Phrase #12

What Would it feel (be) like if ...

Presumes condition is going to take place plus is very non-threatening as it uses "what if". Note: (Feel variation forces a body sensation or feeling or emotion. Remember they are all connected together). --- What would it feel like if you were to instantaneously find yourself completely satisfied by owning this product?"

Conscious By-Pass Phrase #13

As to when

This phrase connects and presupposes the thing will happen. You may wonder as to when or what will trigger all of these teachings to flow naturally from your lips and bring you the pleasures you desire.

Conscious By-Pass Phrase #14

As if

Connector and enhancer. As you look back on reviewing these cards, I invite you to notice how they have already taken effect it's as if you already knew all this stuff and you are enabled and empowered now to do it. Doesn't it just seem natural and great when you look at it that way, NOW.

Conscious By-Pass Phrase #15

If I were to

This is a sneaky way to put ideas or direct focus in the direction you want the conversation to go. If I were to suggest that you can recommend Quantum Selling to everyone you see.

Conscious By-Pass Phrase #16

You Don't Have To

This phrase uses negation which is very powerful because most buyers don't trust sales people. You don't have to believe everything I tell you, just let the logic convince you that this will work great.

Conscious By-Pass Phrase #17

Can You ...

This CBP comes across like the Columbo Effect. "I'm not sure but can you feel good now by imagining owning this product.

Conscious By-Pass Phrase #18

When was the last time

When was the last time you made a good decision on a product similar to this and How did you make that decision?

Conscious By-Pass Phrase #19

When were you best able

This phrase is flexible and wonderful for quickly accessing emotional states which will allow your client to quickly decide on your product. When were you best able to experience complete certainty and pride in realizing that a product like this is perfect for you?

Conscious By-Pass Phrase #20

What Happens As You

Now what happens as you convince yourself that this is the best product for you?

Conscious By-Pass Phrase #21

I Hope You Will

I hope you will refer new customers to me. Now what specifically will cause you to do this?

Trance Word #1

instantaneously

All trance words work because they imply a process that takes place outside of conscious awareness or control. When something happens instantaneously in a person's mind, it's got to come out of an unconscious process.

Trance Word #2

immediately

Again, when you immediately "realize" or "convince yourself" it's happening out of your awareness or control which means T - R - A - N - C - E!

Trance Words #3

find yourself

What does it mean to "find yourself" doing something? That it wasn't consciously planned or executed! Which means

T - R - A - N - C - E!

Trance Words #4

suddenly

Same effect as instantaneously, immediately. It means that the thought comes from another awareness ... the unconscious,

T - R - A - N - C - E!

Trance Words #5

picture

Don't picture yourself having mastered these skills! Picture requires visual internal processing; day dreaming, hallucinating ...
T - R - A - N - C - E!

Trance Words #6

suppose

Suppose you were to master these skills! It means the same thing as "imagine".

T - R - A - N - C - E!

Trance Words #7

convince yourself

Don't convince yourself to master these skills! In order to convince yourself you have to go inside yourself and access all of your internal processes! Very powerful way to induce a

T - R - A - N - C - E

Trance Words #8

realize

When will you realize you can master these skills? To realize means to have a thought just suddenly pop up in your head from your ... unconscious!

T - R - A - N - C - E!

Trance Words #9

ponder

To ponder means to "mull it over" or "think about it", usually in an altered, day-dream type state. In other words

T - R - A - N - C - E!

Trance Words #10

mysterious

For whatever mysterious reason, you might realize suddenly that you can master these skills! Mysterious has shades of unknown, hidden, unconscious,

T - R - A - N - C - E!

Trance Words #11

imagine

It's not important to me that you imagine having mastery of these skills! To imagine requires using your internal processes visually; similar to day dreaming or hallucinating! In other words ...

T - R - A - N - C - E!

Trance Words #12

remember

As you remember a time when you were an exquisite learner, you can realize how easily you can master these skills. Remember means "go inside" and access internally ...

T - R - A - N - C - E!

Trance Words #13

wonder

To wonder requires a state of inner focus, awareness, attention ...
T - R - A - N - C - E!

Trance Words #14

allow

As you allow yourself to master these skills, won't it feel great after you've accomplished it? To allow something means it will happen without conscious effort; in other words unconsciously in

T - R - A - N - C - E!

Trance Words #15

curious

Have you ever been curious as to why and when things just happen? To be curious is to strongly desire to discover what is unknown and making that connection is done in your head.
T - R - A - N - C - E.

Trance Words #16

pretend

Just pretend you are getting all the messages in these cards and that these words are becoming an unconscious part of your vocabulary. To pretend you must go inside and construct something new in

T - R - A - N - C - E.

Trance Words #17

understand

It's only important that you understand what is puzzling only as fast as you master all the Quantum Selling techniques.

Understanding require you to internal process especially if the statement is vague, Ummmmmm, know what I mean.

Trance Words #18

enchant

Have you ever been enchanted by a person, me, I know its happened. To be enchanted you must go inside and enhance those images recalled in euphoria. T - R - A - N - C – E

Trance Words #19

awaken

It's as if you awaken feelings long lost to the point where you become totally alive again. What does it mean to awaken something on the inside of your head. T - R - A - N - C – E

Trance Words #20

What Happens As You

Now what happens as you convince yourself that this is the best product for you?

Most Influential Words

Discover, Good, Money, Easy

I am not going to suggest you will discover just how good this product will fit within your life yet I believe that.

Being able to easily and naturally save money is a guaranteed result, by the product being in your hands ...

Guaranteed, Health, Proven, Results, Value

One can quickly relax, realizing that where there is a guarantee that you can have social health, which will lead to be stress free. Now ...

A customer recently told me that you obviously can see the value by results the product will produce. Because so many people use it, it's proven to get results. It just makes logical sense.

Safe, Save Own, Free, Unique

Our Clients who own this unique course save a tremendous amount of money by simply owning the course and above that they also own a safe assured feeling with this course that gives them security.

When you own this course you can have that feeling of freedom. Free from worry, can you imagine how you now feel as you begin to experience that now.

Best, Love, New, Improved

Notice what it's like as you experience the best feeling that you can have, now when you imagine mastering and loving this course because of the new and improved technology.

Discover and Good

I am not going to suggest you will discover just how good this product will fit within your organization yet I Believe that ...

Money and Easy

Being able to easily and naturally save money is a guaranteed result.

By The Product being in your organization ...

Guaranteed and Health

One can quickly relax, realizing that there is a guarantee that you can have financial health, which will lead to be stress free. Now

Proven and Results

A customer recently told me that you obviously can see that the product will produce results. Because so many people use it, it's proven to get results. It just makes logical sense.

Safe and Save

Our Customers who own this product save a tremendous amount of money by simply owning this product and above that they also own a safe assured feeling with this product that gives them security.

Own and Free

When you own this product you can have that feeling of freedom. Free from worry, can you imagine how you now feel as you begin to experience that now.

Best and Value

Everyone has different opinions and as you start to think about what convinces you that this is the best product on the market, do you focus on value or the good feeling you have by simply owning this product.

Improved and Unique

Notice what it's like as you experience that unique feeling that you can have, now when you imagine owning this product because with those improved feelings of excitement you can ...

Love and New

When was the last time when you really found yourself falling in love with a product, I am sure you can remember that newness of love and all the excitement associated with it and this product can lead you to ...

Process Elicitation #1

How Did You Choose

How did you choose to purchase a product like this in the past.

Process Elicitation #2

What Would Convince You That

What would convince you that this is the best product in the world OR what has convinced you that this is the best product in the World.

Process Elicitation #3

How would you decide/determine that

How do you determine that a product like this, right in front of eyes, is the best thing for you. Hmmmmmm Get it.

Process Elicitation #4

What Caused

What caused you to buy your last product like this one. If they never have bought a product that you represent ask "If you were to decide on a product like this, what would cause you to buy it?

Process Elicitation #5

How Did You Decide To

How did you decide to buy your last product? Once again, if your client hasn't ever bought a product like yours simply Add If you are able to decide on this product How would you do it.

Process Elicitation #6

What would lead you to

What would lead you to refer a new customer to me this second?
You won't call me NOW or will you.

Process Elicitation #7

How Did or Do You Determine That

How do you determine that a product is perfect for you? Like me,
it has to be the best. I believe Quantum Selling is one of those
products. Don't you?

FINISHED FILES ARE THE RESULT OF YEARS OF SCIENTIFIC
STUDY COMBINED WITH THE EXPERIENCE OF MANY YEARS.

Made in the USA
Middletown, DE
04 March 2022

62152369R00086